COMEBACKS
AT WORK

COMEBACKS AT WORK

Using Conversation to Master Confrontation

KATHLEEN KELLEY REARDON, PH.D.,

with Christopher T. Noblet, M.B.A.

HARPER
BUSINESS

An Imprint of HarperCollinsPublishers

HarperCollins books may be purchased for educational, business, or sales promotional use. For information, please write: Special Markets Department, HarperCollins Publishers, 10 East 53rd Street, New York, NY 10022.

FIRST EDITION

Designed by Joy O'Meara

Library of Congress Cataloging-in-Publication Data

Reardon, Kathleen Kelley.
    Comebacks at work : using conversation to master confrontation / by Kathleen Kelley Reardon, Christopher T. Noblet.
        p.   cm.
    ISBN 978-0-06-177102-6
    1. Conflict management. 2. Interpersonal confrontation. 3. Interpersonal communication. 4. Interpersonal conflict. I. Noblet, Christopher T. II. Title.
HD42.R424   2010
650.1'3—dc22   2010015279

10 11 12 13 14   OV/RRD   10 9 8 7 6 5 4 3 2 1

The dearest of friends, Ellen Van Horne Nichols

CONTENTS

AUTHORS' NOTE

Most of the stories and examples that appear in this book come from the authors' interviews and consulting, and so the names of individuals interviewed, as well as the companies they work for, have been changed to protect the identities of those who provided them.

The Art of the Comeback

No doubt you've been put on the spot or cornered in conversation. We all have. Maybe it happened in a discussion you had last week or even yesterday. Perhaps, embarrassed in public, your response just wasn't good enough. You felt somehow inadequate, and angry. You wasted hours—maybe even days—dwelling on the event and rolling it over and over in your mind. You castigated yourself with each and every replay and perhaps ended up hating the person or people whom you held responsible for your disgrace. Then, suddenly in the midst of your unrelenting misery, it came to you. "I should have said . . ." But it's too late now. All you can do is wonder: "Why didn't I think of that then?"

The answer is simple. If you find yourself in this kind of situation often, you didn't think of saying the effective thing because you haven't yet mastered the art of the comeback. You're not alone. And the good news is that this condition is only temporary.

No one is born a comeback expert. It takes trial and error, adherence to a set of principles about communication, and practice with an array of options. What it *doesn't* require is that you be someone other than yourself—just a more astute version. And don't expect to turn into a communication pro overnight. The most expert among us, even those people who seem to know what to say under any and all circumstances, still have their *"If only I'd said"* moments.

WHAT THIS BOOK WILL DO FOR YOU

The goal of this book is to render those situations rare for you. While it's useful to have a list of quips ready to use when you're in a tight spot (and you'll find some of those here), learning to distinguish between types of situations is important, too. When, for example, should you give back as good as you got? When should you cut someone some slack? And what are all the stages in between? Essentially, you'll learn how to handle a variety of situations and, in so doing, avoid reliving them in the future.

We'll begin by looking at what comebacks are, and at the typical obstacles that stand in the way of people dealing with them effectively. We're all responsible for how others treat us because we're part of any communication with them. If we commonly let insults pass that should be addressed, we are telling other people that they can walk all over us with impunity. That's not good. So in this book we advance, early on, the perspective that what happens to us at work is usually due to what we allow or disallow.

Since all of us are creatures of habit, the way we communicate often becomes unsurprising, and this in itself can get us into trouble. If you are completely predictable at work, anyone can manage you, whether a boss, a colleague, or someone who works for you. We tackle that problem in the first four chapters of this book. You need to get in charge of what happens to you at work, and that includes not allowing people to know how they can anger, hurt, bully, dupe, or in some other way maneuver you to their liking.

Chapter 5 looks at why so many of us draw a mental blank when we run into situations that call for comebacks. Why do we freeze up? What is it that allows us—hours later—to think of what we should have said but didn't when the time was right? We'll show you how you can get rid of that tendency and free yourself to consider a host of comeback options.

A good part of being able to identify and employ comebacks with comfort is having a set of them available to you. So, even if you already have some of your own, we introduce in chapter 6 the "R-List": a set of ten types of comebacks that you can begin to experiment with today. Among these strategies, you'll learn to reframe, restate, and retaliate, and you can keep all ten techniques in mind or in your desk for those times when you need help.

In chapter 7 we look at the role that gut instinct plays in comebacks. We all have gut instincts, but we don't always trust them—sometimes with good reason. How can you nurture your own instinct to a point where you'll feel sufficiently confident to let it help you choose and execute good comebacks? To assist you with this, we will introduce a way of looking at the rational and "gut" aspects of every comeback decision and of determining whether one or the other will likely bring about the best results. Additionally, the most effective comebacks are not without passion, so we'll also explore in this chapter how emotions and body language contribute to the skilled comeback equation.

In chapter 8 we'll focus on how to use comebacks when conflict is inevitable, and we'll especially look at how to avoid making a situation personal that doesn't need to be. In other words, we'll explore when to insert ourselves into a comeback and when to be objective. This will continue to develop your ability to select better comebacks.

There is, however, no such thing as a comeback that, no matter how clever, works with all people and in all settings. That is why the next two chapters are about how to "read" conversation partners and situations. Chapter 9 will teach you how to take people's pulse, so to speak, and to determine which types of comebacks are likely to work with them. We then explore in chapter 10 how situations dictate parameters that make some types of comebacks too risky and others more likely to succeed.

Establishing your comfort zone comes next. You'll learn to develop a host of comebacks and have them ready to use. These will be ones that are your own and that you know you can use because they fit who you are. Along with those, you'll have a set of comebacks that take you outside your comfort zone for those times when someone's rudeness or crudeness exceeds your threshold.

Along the way, the chapters include methods of testing yourself and organizing what is introduced in each chapter, while chapter 11 introduces a self-assessment technique that will help you condense what you have learned in a way that facilitates recollection when you need to use comebacks in the future. By asking yourself the ten questions featured in the final chapter, you will be better prepared to use more effective comebacks the next time you're put on the spot.

I've spent my career teaching and training people to communicate more effectively. By providing a range of possibilities for a variety of situations, I will draw upon that experience to help you locate what works best for you. Together, we'll look also at using comebacks effectively in situations outside of the workplace, because to become proficient at comebacks, it's important to know how to employ them effectively in a variety of contexts. Occasionally, too, we'll look at how comebacks are used in politics, or when negotiating an important purchase, or even when dealing with annoying behaviors of friends or neighbors. You'll find that these examples can be applied to work as well. By the end of the book, as if you and I had had several private sessions together, you'll be on your way to mastering confrontation and taking control of how people treat you, and you'll be much more in charge of what happens to you at work than ever before.

CHAPTER ONE

Why Communication Matters

Before moving on to look specifically at comebacks, it'll be useful to take a few minutes to talk about how communication works and why it matters. That is the foundation for all that follows, and the best place to start is in our brains, where the thoughts we communicate, poorly or well, originate.

Science has provided substantial evidence for the *neuroplasticity* of our brains. We now know, for example, about the human brain's considerable capacity to adapt to change and to compensate for accident or illness. There are pathways that can be forged by a threatened brain that were never used before or, for that matter, that didn't even exist. But we've also learned that in the absence of such threats, our brains will often go merrily along, operating on a small percentage of their capacity. An unprovoked or lazy brain—which most of us have—doesn't reach beyond its comfort zone. And that's exactly how many of us communicate.

A lazy brain affects our communication in negative ways. Far fewer interaction pathways are identified and utilized. When we don't provoke ourselves to learn creative ways of handling difficult situations, we fall into patterns and consider them adequate. If you have a lazy brain, you may either avoid conflict or slip into argumentativeness at the slightest hint of criticism. Or maybe you incline toward acting in the same way over and over with certain people, and then see problems as their fault. We all engage in some of these and other types of dysfunctional patterns. These patterns are a good part of the reason why comebacks don't come easily to most people.

Communication is less about what somebody says to you than about how you receive that message and what you do about it. If you try to think of communication in terms of a game of chess, your responsibility becomes clear. In chess you don't just let the other player lead you around the board, or play the game the same way over and over even though you've lost each time. If you want to start winning, you do some leading and strategizing yourself. With practice, you come to see that each of your moves limits your opponent's further options, just as his moves limit yours. Both of you have "input" into the outcome. The person who abdicates his part of that input almost always loses.

While we don't tend to think of most types of communication in terms of victories and defeats, effective communication does require strategic involvement. It's a matter of learning over time, by trial and error. And to the extent that you haven't been learning and practicing comebacks, your job and career can suffer.

Consider, for example, the experience of Stephen Kepler, a chemical-industry communications manager who was attending a meeting with two senior managers and the vice chairman of his company. Problems had arisen with how some sensitive information had been made public. Before the communications manager could even open his mouth to speak, a senior vice president known for his fierce temper proceeded to, in Kepler's words, "rip me up one side and down the other for failing to get the proper approval to release the information." The senior manager continued his assault for what seemed like an eternity. He pointed at Kepler, pounded on the table, and then waved a copy of the offending material inches from Kepler's nose.

Kepler might have defended himself immediately. Instead, he sat silently, intensely uncomfortable, his blood pressure rising. He hardly blinked as he bore the angry onslaught. He made himself hold back. Finally, after tossing Kepler's way a few more insults, a look of disgust, and a final re-insistence that he should have gotten approval before releasing the sensitive information, the senior vice president stopped speaking and simply glared, waiting for an abject apology. Instead, Kepler looked straight-faced at the executive, placed a hand on the document that had been waved with such incivility moments before, and simply said: "I had the approval." Then he opened the document and pointed to the signed approval.

If you had been Stephen Kepler what would you have done? Would you have interrupted the executive early on in his rant? Kepler chose not to take that course. He did not cower, nor did he allow his facial expression to reveal the range of intense emotion he'd been feeling as people who could decide his future at the company watched his career seem to derail before their eyes. Kepler could have shouted back at the irate senior manager who was so full of himself and his power. He might have interrupted the SVP with a clever remark, actively showing him up for a loud buffoon. However, instead of humiliating his attacker, he let that person humiliate himself.

Later that day, the vice president actually apologized to Kepler for the treatment he had undergone at the meeting. Kepler graciously accepted the apology and returned to his work. Not long afterward, he had to work again with the SVP who'd unfairly berated him. Interestingly, that man appeared to have learned something from the way Kepler had coolly and evenly handled what could have been a devastating experience with long-lasting consequences. The two of them ultimately found a way forward by putting the issue behind them.

Not everyone could have appeared as patient and confident as

Stephen Kepler. In fact, most people would have reacted much earlier, and more strongly. Observing that his attacker was way out of line, and sensing he was being used as a scapegoat, Kepler had no qualms about letting his attacker dig an ever larger hole for himself. His comeback was masterful not only because of its timing and restraint, but also owing to the calmness with which it was delivered.

Compare this to a similar meeting that took place at an insurance company on the other side of the country. Public relations project managers Paul Romano and Linda Bromley were working on an assignment for one of the company's product divisions—a project that was running into some problems and obstacles. They sat down for a progress review with Allison Werner, a team member from the product division, as well as with Allison's VP boss and the division's senior VP. Fairly new at the company, Romano had never before met either of these senior managers.

No sooner had the meeting gotten under way than Werner launched into a vehement diatribe, blaming every difficulty on the PR department. She said, "They're not getting the material to us on time, so we can't get anything done." She continued in this vein, taking none of the responsibility, and building up a head of steam.

Romano stopped her in her tracks. "I didn't let her go for a minute after she got rolling," Romano told me. "My blood pressure was up and I was showing it. My face must have turned completely red. I put my arm out to stop her and then insisted emphatically, 'That's not true!'" Werner was stunned. She hadn't expected someone to return an attack on her turf in front of her bosses. "I was sure," Romano recalled, "that she expected me, a newbie, to keep my mouth shut and take my medicine." "Why didn't you?" I asked. He told me, "I'm just not that kind of person. I wasn't about to sit there and let her tell lies about my work."

Romano turned to the senior executives and explained that PR had been getting the materials to Werner's division on time and in accurate form. Indeed, he told them, it was her division holding things up. "It's not something I'd ever done before," Romano said. "But I was thinking to myself, 'I'm not taking this,' and I didn't. Maybe if I'd known the senior execs, I would have rolled my eyes, or done something like that, but she'd gone from teammate to enemy in two seconds flat. I wasn't going to sit there and take that."

Over the following years, Romano worked with the senior executives, and his comeback hadn't damaged his standing with them. He even worked a couple of times with Werner. She remained "distant and cautious," Romano remembered. "But she never gave me any more trouble." He added, "From that point I never let anyone inaccurately and publicly challenge my work. They wouldn't get ten seconds into it before I'd say, 'Hey. That's not true.'"

As his career continued, Romano was usually the low guy on the totem pole in meetings. He tended to be with the CEO and other high-status people but he told me, " I never stood still for public pillorying even from them."

These are two similar stories, with important differences. Kepler waited, as difficult as it was, to calmly deliver his comeback. Romano responded immediately. In both cases, they knew they were right. They knew they were being used to deflect blame away from their detractors. One was a "newbie," the other well along in his career, though not yet a senior manager. They both could have ruined their careers in their respective companies on the spot. Instead, because of their conviction, manner of delivery, and the way their comebacks suited their different personal styles, each benefited from saying what he knew to be true, albeit at different points in time in the conflicts.

These kinds of public insults happen sooner or later to people at work, and it doesn't matter if that work happens to be singing in the church choir. If you don't know how to respond effectively to situations in which your character or ability is hung out to dry, you're going to get burned.

That outcome is going to become less and less likely as you read the following chapters. Just knowing that there are many ways to respond to the people with whom you work, and to the situations you face is a big step forward in itself. As you become aware of obstacles in your path and begin removing them, comebacks will come to you more naturally, and people will begin to think twice before making you their target.

CHAPTER TWO

Getting Started

Unless you're very fortunate, many of the types of scenarios below have happened or will happen to you at work:

You offer a suggestion and once again a colleague dismisses it as something tried before that won't work now.

Your boss is clearly wrong, but she is rarely receptive to criticism or advice.

At an after-work social gathering you're asked personal questions about your salary and the cost of your home.

You walk into a meeting and the person who's after your job quips, "Look who decided to join us."

You've hired a talented person who seems to be mistaking your professional admiration for something more.

An idea you introduce gets no traction until it's introduced a half hour later by someone who treats it as his.

Your boss assigns you yet another thankless, dead-end task.

Just at the moment when you are making an important point, a detractor cracks a joke at your expense.

Your name is mysteriously left off a report on which you did a lot of work.

Countless people drive to work each day wondering whether they'll be facing situations like these. They worry that they'll be caught off guard, taken for granted, used, abused, or cornered. They know how to do their basic jobs well, and even expertly, but they haven't learned what to say and do to *save* those jobs and their credibility when they're put on the spot. When things get tough, such people experience the awful feeling that they are losing control and their careers are sinking.

What do you say, for example, if your boss tells you that you're extremely accomplished but adds, "We don't see you as having leadership potential"? This happens often, and most people don't know what to say. They think, as one senior executive shared with me, "I don't know how he can say that. After all, I've done so much more than he has in my career. Besides, what was he talking about, anyway? What does he mean by 'leadership potential'? He can't lead to save his life, yet he's my boss!"

When comments about "leadership potential," or some other supposedly valued but vague or undefined concept, are made to diminish someone, they often have little connection to reality. There's no use torturing yourself looking for the logic because it's likely not in the words themselves. It's important to realize that a comment about a lack of leadership potential can be another way of saying, "We don't think you're a good fit" or "We don't want to promote you because you're not one of us." So pulling your hair out and struggling to find the logic in such a comment or listing all the reasons why you *are* a good leader is not likely to be productive.

I learned early in my career that arguing whether or not something is fair at work is usually a waste of time. Many good, responsible people grow up valuing certain ways of being and acting that are easily trumped at work by the often supposed importance of a collective mission. "We're running a business here, not a charity" and "It's not personal, it's business" are used to justify unfairness in many organizations. For those who want to get rid of someone or justify refusal of a promotion, there's always, "We don't see you as a team player." It works even if they hired you to work alone in a cubicle all day because common wisdom in business places a higher value on teamwork than individual needs or concerns. Here I might mention that this rule is, of course, often not applied when it comes to determining the salaries and perks given to senior management. And so, as I said, most of the time it's not really a rule; it's an excuse for treating someone unfairly.

What should you say to such work "truisms"? That depends on a number of things, including your relationship with the person who said it, and whether you're the only two people present. Rather than say nothing and walk away with steam coming out of your ears, why not ask for more detail? For example, "What would you say is the most important characteristic of a team player?"

Questions are used as comebacks far less often than they should be. We'll look at this more closely later on. For now, it's good to know that when in doubt about what's actually being said, or to buy some time, questions are very useful. They make the other person do some work. They prevent you from walking away from a capricious label without having expressed at least some discomfort or resistance.

Here are a couple of possible responses to the accusation of lacking leadership potential:

"It would be instructive to know which specific leadership attributes got you where you are today."

"Some people are commanding leaders. I prefer not to lead that way. I'm more of a motivational leader."

"Leadership is a complex concept. Which aspects are we talking about here?"

If the person applying the label has done so without thinking it through, he or she will have some difficulty providing a specific response. Not that many people question comments like, "You lack leadership potential" or "We don't see you as a team player." They respond as if it's sufficiently meaningful to not require further discussion. The person who made the comment usually expects the recipient to go home and fret about which leadership attributes he or she lacks. When you don't do that, it's unsettling for them. And that's useful, because a comeback that unsettles a conversation usually gives the person who initiated that statement some time to think and to open up some avenues for persuasion.

More often than not, comebacks are statements or expressions that restore some degree of balance when the recipient has been insulted, embarrassed, demeaned, ignored, or in some other way challenged in conversation. Sometimes the balance restored is one of power. At other times equanimity is returned to a relationship threatened by something one party said. Of course, some comebacks are so proficient that they flip the power. These are so effective that the person who did the insulting or caused the embarrassment finds himself worse off for having done so.

We acquire the skill to use comebacks over time. However, in this book we're going to speed up the learning process by covering what it takes to be able to think on your feet in difficult situations and also what types of responses work best for you. That's the beauty of communication—and another way that it's like chess. There are many ways to achieve the same goal.

When someone hurls an insult at you, for example, you can decide to "hear" it instead as an errant comment and thus completely alter the direction of the interaction, and even your relationship. This might be the case with a person who is a poor communicator but has other redeeming features. So you decide to give her a break this time. You may also have more pressing issues on your plate right now and so avoiding an altercation is best for you at the moment. Perhaps you know that she really meant to say something different, but she jumbled her words or neglected to think sufficiently before saying them. Or she may just be someone who does this kind of thing all the time, and dignifying her offensiveness by giving her the fight she's looking for simply isn't productive for you.

As an example, imagine someone saying this to you:

"That's one of the most stupid ideas I've ever heard."

By nearly any standard of interpretation, this is insulting. But you could decide not to take it that way, and instead reply:

"I thought the same thing at first, but you'll find it quite ingenious if you listen a bit longer."

Or, you might say:

" 'Stupid' is exactly what people usually think of innovative ideas."

Another option:

"That's a natural first reaction."

If you want to address the insult more directly but still avoid having the conversation deteriorate into an argument, the following can be useful:

> "I could take that personally, but I'm in a good mood today and this project is too important."

Such responses let the person know you're not pleased by his choice of words while also taking the conversation in a positive direction. Each is a response rather than a knee-jerk, in-kind reaction.

Adept communicators begin each day knowing that they need not be the victims of how other people speak to them. They understand, as we'll soon discuss, how they are in large part responsible for the outcome of every conversation—as well as for the nature of the relationships—they have at work.

THE 75 PERCENT RULE

If we see most of life's events as available for interpretation, then avenues of opportunity will open before us. Similar to the example above about redirecting an insult, we can interpret what people say in ways that suit our own goals. Former president Bill Clinton believes that most of life is "how you respond to what's happening, not what's happening."

There's a distinction here that's very important. We needn't totally fool ourselves or let others get away with gratuitous attacks. Instead, when it behooves us to do so, we can decide how best to interpret what's happening to us and then use that interpretation to guide our choices.

In the following interaction, there are several opportunities for interpretation. And it's not so much what is said here, or even how it's said, but how each person involved decides to interpret what they see and hear.

> Elise: Don't tell me you're *still* working on that same report!
> Alec: Okay. I won't tell you that.
> Elise: Seriously. You've been obsessing on it since this morning.
> Alec: And you're bothered about this because . . . ?
> Elise: It's just odd. I mean, you do this all the time.
> Alec: It's unusual. But it's gotten me this far.

You've likely experienced the colleague who can't help commenting on the way you do your job. If he or she doesn't say something like the first comment above, they are bound to find something else to bug you about. You could get angry, sputter, dwell on it all day, and even take it home to ponder. Why not employ an interpretation that allows you to address the issue in a way that doesn't encourage your colleague to continue bothering you—one that ends the discussion, leaving him or her wondering what happened, and that lets you get your work done? It's much more effective than letting such people get to you and thereby waste your time.

Employing this kind of communication management is what I've described in the past as the 75 Percent Rule: **Each of us is at least 75 percent responsible for how people respond to us.** Let someone else say and do what they might, we still influence how our conversations proceed. We have a proprietary interest in how our conversations turn out at work because each one is a building block of our careers. Each conversation contributes to how others see us and how we see ourselves. It tells other people what they can get away with and what they can't. To the extent that we abdicate that 75 percent responsibility, we give others power to decide our futures. And that can't be good.

There are multiple places in any conversation where one of the parties can change how things are going. In the interaction above, "Don't tell me you're *still* working on that report" is undoubtedly spoken as a criticism. But note that Alec doesn't accept or treat it as one. He replies to the comment as a request and answers it as such by saying, "Okay. I won't tell you that." Elise then tries to continue with her initial barrage of disparagement. At this point, Alec could become annoyed or angry at her use of the word "obsession." Instead, he elects to ask her why she's so interested. When she insists on being critical by labeling his actions as "odd" and something he "does all the time," Alec bypasses the latter criticism and redefines "odd" as "unusual" (a more positive way to describe the same thing). At this point, Elise's options become limited. She's getting nowhere in her attempts to belittle or annoy Alec. She may walk away shaking her head, but at least Alec is rid of her. She is more likely to think twice before trying again to unsettle him, because he has followed the 75 Percent Rule and demonstrated that he's not an easy mark for critics like her.

How do people get into the frame of mind that enables them to ignore insults and redirect a conversation toward a quick end or in some constructive way? Dan Gilbert, author of *Stumbling on Happiness*, believes that humans have psychological immune systems that help us change our view of the world when the present one is not working well for us. We can "synthesize" happiness, he proposes, even in the midst of some miserable circumstances. We can find a silver lining and provide ourselves a positive vantage point from which to operate in life. Alec (above) doesn't synthesize happiness, but he does create a view that allows him to address only those parts of Elise's comments that would avoid combat and allow him to return to his work.

When communicating, we can decide to see what is happening to us in a variety of ways. We can create a positive sense of a situation even when most observers would expect it to end badly. We can answer sarcastic questions, for example, as if they are simply objective inquiries. Smiling slightly before doing so may let the person asking the question sense that you likely caught the sarcastic drift, but chose to move on. This can work quite effectively and makes them think twice about trying it again. Ridiculous comments can be construed as, oddly, quite appropriate and even insightful if there is some redeeming element to be found within them. When taking questions after a speech, if people ask questions that seem oddly out of context, I try to find a way to make them relevant. Or if they challenge me in an inappropriate way, perhaps more vehemently than the topic should elicit, I try here, too, to find an element of reason to which I can connect my response. It saves face for them if the audience appears to think they're out of line and makes a positive situation out of a potentially negative one.

An insult can be treated as humor by laughing when the other person expects you to retaliate. The meaning you choose to tease out of a potentially negative conversation or a relationship-threatening comment can be more important to how things proceed than the original intent of your would-be detractor.

Chris, the coauthor of this book, was out bicycling recently when he observed a boy of about eight years trying to learn to ride without training wheels. Each time his father gave him a shove and let go, the boy became audibly upset, lost his balance, and stopped. Frustrated, he shouted, "I'm never going to be a good bike rider!" His little sister, who was cycling quite well on two wheels herself, called out to him:

"The more you scream, the more you lean!"

How about that for an on-the-spot, 75 percent responsible piece of advice? And from a six-year-old! And it worked, too. Her brother got back on his bike and kept trying, recognizing that his success was at least partially his own responsibility and that he'd best get on with it.

All of us could benefit from remembering "The more you scream, the more you lean," because, in general, handling tough situations at work requires a lot more observing and considering than complaining and blaming. It's about getting on with it and taking our share of the responsibility for making things go well.

It's true, as with the difference between the little girl and her brother, that a mild aggravation for one person can be a crisis of great magnitude for another. What comes as a natural skill to one person may not come easily at all to someone else. In nearly all cases, though, how we "frame" a situation—how we choose to define what is going on—affects how we fare in it. If you're sensitive to criticism, it's difficult to change that. But you can change what you decide *is* criticism. That's a very important skill.

If you know, for example, that you're dealing with a bully, it helps. Bullies are small people who are seeking power at your expense. Why encourage them? When you just can't let pass what they've said, dismissing their power can often prove effective:

"You're known for going too far, but this time you're way out of your league."

"You know, I'm going to let that pass because you've done enough damage to yourself without my input."

"You're nothing if not predictable."

In later chapters we'll sort out when a situation calls for a direct, reciprocal comeback. Most of the time, it's of little use to stoop to the level of a bully. Instead, it often pays to "take the high road" and refuse to accept an insult as it was intended.

While we were writing this book, homemaking mogul Martha Stewart commented on the comparative competence of television chef Rachael Ray in a way that could easily have been taken by Ray as a put-down. Specifically, in an interview with Cynthia McFadden of ABC News's *Nightline* broadcast in November 2009, Stewart had said of Ray:

> *She professed she cannot bake. She just did a new cookbook, which is just a re-edit of her old recipes. That's not good enough for me. I mean, I really want to write a book that is a unique and lasting thing, something that will really fulfill a need in someone's library. So, she's different. She's more of an entertainer . . . with a bubbly personality than she is a teacher like me.*

Few would have blamed Rachael Ray for reacting negatively to this comment. It was treated in the media as a public trashing of Ray. But Ray either didn't see it that way initially or, on second thought, refused to do so. Instead of focusing on what Stewart was implying, Ray chose to publicly interpret the content as though Stewart had simply made an understandable observation. When pressed by the feud-baiting *Nightline* for a reaction, Ray replied:

> *Why would it make me mad? Her skill set is far beyond mine. That's simply the reality of it. That doesn't mean that what I do isn't important too. I just think she's being honest. When it comes to producing a beautiful, perfect, high-quality meal, I'd rather eat Martha's than mine.*

Now, that was impressive!

The figure below shows some of the options Ray had for what many people would have perceived as an insult, even if accidentally so. If we take Stewart's words as promoted by the press—as an insult—the model below shows how Ray skillfully avoided perma-nent harm to her relationship with Stewart by choosing to bypass that definition and by reframing Stewart's comments.

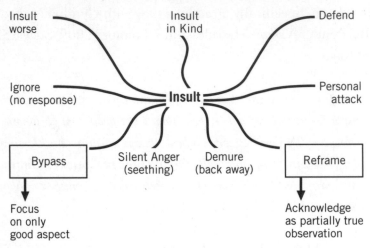

Without necessarily thinking of it in this way, Ray divided what Stewart said into parts she would address and those she would ignore or bypass. The first included reference to Ray having "professed" to not being able to bake and to having written a book that is just a reedit of past writing. Had Ray reacted to these comments alone, the outcome would have been quite different. Instead, Ray bypassed the implied insult. She did the same with Stewart's descriptions of herself as wanting to provide people with something enduring for their libraries, which implied that Ray's book is inferior. Here again, Ray did not directly defend herself by saying, "My books are every bit as enduring and have an equal place in people's libraries." Instead, she took the gist of Stewart's comments to that point as Stewart's well-deserved compliment to herself. By so doing, Ray removed the element of personal slight. It allowed Ray to reply graciously, "Why would it make me mad? Her skill set is far beyond mine. That's just the reality of it." In other words, that Stewart was simply making a factual observation.

Of course, such a statement was much more than just gracious, but Ray likely had a goal in mind: "Let's put this behind us and move on." Moreover, Ray did address the implication that Stewart's level of skill somehow makes that which Ray does not valuable. This was important; if she'd simply been gracious and acted as if there wasn't an iota of slight in Stewart's words, Ray's response surely would have seemed disingenuous or motivated by her fear of Martha. By saying "That doesn't mean what I do isn't important," she addressed that part of what had been said that needed to be corrected. She stood up for herself without issuing a counter-insult.

She finished with a "reframing." Although Stewart had never mentioned whose house people would rather visit for dinner or who cooks a better meal, Ray made that the focus—and claimed that even she would prefer to go to Stewart's home for dinner. Martha Stewart's home would be perfectly decorated and the whole experience would be special. One might derive from this that Ray "doesn't do perfect" and that her viewers don't look for the same level of perfection in their entertaining, from stemware to wall decoration, that is invariably depicted on Stewart's show. So Ray's compliment conceded to Stewart a corner where she is unquestionably more proficient. It brought what could have been a series of back-and-forth insults in the scandal media to a positive end.

This is a very useful, public example of what communication-conflict experts call "fractionation"—dividing up the contentious remarks into manageable pieces and then responding to the bits that best suit your needs.

Of course, if they'd been together on the same television set when Stewart had made her comment, it might have been much harder for Ray to come up with a response that defused the situation so effectively. Nevertheless, her response demonstrates how focusing on what others may see as the obvious intention in someone's comments is often not the best option. Ray didn't lose anything by refusing to respond with an insult. Instead, she showed herself to be quite confident, intelligent, and generous.

In your own interactions, taking the high road, as Ray did, comes with practice. To become capable of managing 75 percent of what happens to you requires considerable knowledge about yourself and about the types of responses you can carry off well. In some respects it's a journey—one where feedback from your friends, relatives, colleagues, teachers, and bosses can be invaluable, even if not always positive—as you progress. We're all creatures of pattern, and an important part of changing for the better is to learn to recognize our patterns and to alter those that are dysfunctional.

The important lesson at this juncture is to be aware that there's usually more than one effective way to think about and respond to challenges in conversation. Developing such awareness will be a strong start toward taking more charge of what happens to you each day. Then you'll begin to have input into how your relationships evolve and are maintained. In this way, you influence the course of your career.

RECOGNIZING CLUES THAT SOMETHING IS AMISS

Here's some good news in the quest to manage what happens to us: We're not starting from scratch. We enter into conversations relying on some guidelines that we've been learning for years: rules concerning how communication is supposed to go in all cultures. We learn them growing up. So most of the day we can enter into conversations without having to watch our every word. Being creatures of pattern, and having all been socialized in similar ways, we can expect, for example, that friendliness will be greeted with at least some degree of friendliness in return. A gracious "Hello" is supposed to be received as a signal to reciprocate in kind. When that doesn't happen, we can either brush it off or take it as a possible clue that something is amiss.

We all have memories of episodes when people didn't act as we would have preferred or expected. In those memories there are also recollections of warning signals that we may or may not have heeded at the time. In previous writing, I've referred to those as "red alerts," signals to stop and pay attention as something is happening here that isn't quite right, or that isn't safe. When we see or hear those signals in the present time, they may not trigger a complete recollection, but if we're fortunate they at least cause us to pause and reflect.

Those people who always blame other persons or blame the situation for what happens to them, I'm convinced, don't learn these cues as effectively as do people who are more inclined toward what psychologist Jules Rotter called an "internal locus of control."[1] To have an internal locus of control is to see yourself as the causal agent of much of what happens to you. If we incline *too* far in that direction, however, we won't learn either, because we'll be overwhelmed with the blame we place on ourselves when things go wrong. We need enough of an internal locus of control to ask ourselves what we just did or didn't do (or did or didn't attend to) that led us to the place we didn't want to go. If you fail to make this kind of assessment on a regular basis when things don't go well, you're depriving yourself of the benefits of what could later become "gut feelings" that something is amiss. If you rarely or never look back to review and assess what happened before conversational problems arose—clues you might learn to heed in the future—then you're going wrong. And you can change that. This important step in comeback self-training requires a shift of attention away from simply pressing forward in a conversation that's going wrong, a shift toward trying to understand what just happened and from there—and with the knowledge from past experience—moving in more productive directions.

Becoming good at comebacks, then, requires learning from mistakes and missed opportunities. It wouldn't hurt at this point to think of a time in the not-too-distant past when you didn't heed cues that someone was about to put you on the spot. Perhaps this person tried to embarrass you or derail you from expressing your thoughts clearly. He or she may have used you as the butt of a joke. In any case, now that you think back, could you have seen it coming and gotten out of the way? Could you have set the conversation on a track that would have precluded the attack? Was there something in his or her tone of voice, for example, that you knew usually occurs when this person is about to belittle someone?

That is the kind of thing that people who are good at comebacks tend to notice. They can sense when someone is about to try to trip them up in some way or use them for their own benefit. So they're poised, perhaps not with exactly what words they'll say but with a fair idea of how they might respond. Good comebacks rarely come out of the blue. Many have been learned in a prior occasion and practiced as well. We'll discuss this more in subsequent chapters, but it's useful to start thinking about cues. Pay attention to the conversations you have or hear over the next day or two, looking only for signs that someone at work is about to put you or someone else on the spot. Once you get good at this, it's difficult for such people to catch you off guard.

This chapter has been about the first steps in learning to become proficient at comebacks. Largely its focus has been on how much control we really can have if we pay attention and manage ourselves instead of allowing others to manage us.

To review, it may help to ask yourself these questions:

More often than not—

1. Have I been thinking of conversations as building blocks of my career, which I can influence, or have I just been letting them happen to me?
2. Do I react more than respond when facing a challenge in conversation?
3. Am I flexible? Is there plasticity in my communication, or do I slip into ruts easily? Am I too predictable?
4. Do I regularly take a dysfunctional conversation on to a more productive path by attending to the parts that serve my goals best?
5. Am I at or near the seventy-five percent level of responsibility for my communication? Or do I tend to let other people limit my choices—like an amateur chess player only thinking of the next turn?
6. Am I attentive to clues in conversation that something is about to become a challenge? Do I pay attention to what usually comes before these kinds of situations so I'm more ready for them in the future?

Your answers will suggest some things to begin working on *now* toward becoming at least 75 percent responsible for what happens to you each day. Try today to direct a conversation in ways you haven't tried before. When you're inclined to silence in the face of insult, or to reacting negatively, try turning the situation around to your favor by not letting habit dictate how your respond.

No matter where you start, by the end of this book you will be more adept than you've ever been before at making sure that you are not pushed and pulled through life but rather that you do a considerable amount of pushing and pulling of your own.

CHAPTER THREE

Assessing Your Baseline Comeback Skill

Having established that each of us is at least 75 percent responsible for how people treat us at work, the next step is to do a little stretching in preparation for learning when to say what to whom in a spontaneous way. The best way to start is with a kind of pre-study quiz. Why not establish how effective you are now at coming up with what to say in situations that tend to happen regularly at work? So, we start this chapter with a scenario and comeback options to choose from. It will get you thinking about how to sort out the situations that require a strong direct response from those that benefit from a more indirect one.

Think in terms of reserving at least 75 percent control of the situation for yourself. Watch out for reactions. They're impulsive and, therefore, often not effective. Responses, on the other hand, involve reasoned, more thoughtful actions. They aren't always effective, but the odds are greater of their being so—especially if you follow the steps below in formulating them.

BEGINNING YOUR ASSESSMENT

To help you with this baseline assessment of your skill, first consider locating your sense of the situation along the continuums below:

Accidental _____ Intentional

Slight Offense _____Insult

There are many more categories to consider when formulating a comeback, but starting with these two is helpful. If a comment in question seems more accidental than intentional and also falls at the "slight offense" end of the second continuum, then an intense, direct response is unnecessary. Of course, we would need to know how often this person does this kind of thing, more about the relationship and situation, but we'll add that kind of information in future chapters. Relying largely on the two continuums above, let's look at the first situation:

> *You are asked by a colleague to stay late in order to complete a project. Normally you would, and you certainly have many times before, but this time you have very important plans. The project deadline is several days from now and you believe his tendency to have to be early all the time shouldn't mean your plans must be canceled. You tell him that you won't be able to stay. He asks why. You say, "It's family related." To your surprise, given how well you've worked together in the past and your considerable efforts to accommodate his anxiety about time, he then says, "If you can't pull your own weight on these team projects, you should say so up front so I don't have to suffer the consequences. I have a family, too, but you don't see me shirking my responsibilities here."*

Where would you place this colleague's remarks on the accidental/intentional and the slight offense/insult continuums? Where you place what he said on these is critical in determining how you respond. Once you do that, you should also, as demonstrated in the Martha Stewart–Rachael Ray scenario in chapter 2, think about your goal. Let's say you need to work with this person in the future. And you'd prefer to do so in an amicable manner. But you also don't want him to get the message that he can insult you with no ramifications.

Let's say you decide his comments were somewhere toward the intentional side. You believe he should have known better. His words may have struck you as somewhat manipulative—using a failure to be a team player to get you to do what he wants. Maybe he's tired. But that's no excuse.

On the insult continuum, you might place his comments, again, somewhere in the middle. You're taken aback by this sudden disparagement of your work. Had he not impugned your sense of responsibility and commitment to the team, you might have considered his reaction more of a slight offense caused by anxiety over the project completion.

These placements tell you that this person has gone a bit too far. He surprised you, so he isn't a serial offender, but he should have considered all the times you've stayed late at his request before attempting to disparage your decision.

Where you actually placed this situation on the two continuums may differ. But keeping your goal in mind and using these points for now, which of the following comebacks would work best?

A. "Every time you've asked, I've stayed late. I can't believe you think that not doing so one time means I'm not a team player."

B. "Who died and made you king?"

C. "This time I'm going to pretend I didn't hear the second part of what you said. Let's meet early tomorrow and stay late if need be. Tonight I'm busy."

D. "Maybe if you had a life, you wouldn't be so quick to judge other people's priorities."

E. "If you talk to me like that again, it's not me who'll be looking for a different team to work with."

Take a moment to arrange these in order of preference. You may have a really good one of your own, but practicing with just these for now, which ones are better? Before continuing to read, take a moment to rank the above options in order of effectiveness.

Order of Priority: _____

_____

_____

_____

_____

None of these is a terrible response, but A is far too defensive. Yes, it does let the offender know that you've stayed often in the past. But as the first words out of your mouth, it's just too weak, given where his comments were on the intentionality and insult ranges. Whenever you hear yourself using "I" more than once, watch out. You're likely making the situation about you and what you did or did not do wrong. This situation should be about what he did wrong. Later on you can remind him of your commitment to the team on all previous occasions, but for now you need to say something that makes him stop and think about his choice of words.

"Who died and made you king?" isn't bad under the circumstances, depending on how it's said. Let's say it's delivered without evident anger. It's then a question that might bring him up short and cause him to think about how he made himself the "better worker" of the two of you and the decider. It's his way or the highway. In some businesses, this would work, but it's difficult to avoid delivering this one without sounding flippant and so probably works better in high school than at work. And just as choice A made the whole situation about you, choice B made it all about him and provides no reasoning or reasonable outcome.

Choice D is too strong under the circumstances. It's asking for an altercation, while your goal is to return the situation to normalcy. It's way too personal. Yes, he took a swipe at your work commitment, but you're countering with a swipe at his entire life. Why escalate in this way, given your goal and the level of intentionality and insult? It's a reaction, not a response. It's one of those win-the-battle-but-lose-the-war options.

Choice E is a threat. And while it's understandable that someone might react this way, threats are rarely effective comebacks, and they often escalate an already bad situation. A board director for one of the largest and most successful U.S. retailers put it this way: "Generally it's not a good idea to come back at someone with threats. You don't reestablish authority. You only relieve feelings." It can be useful to relieve your feelings, but doing so by threat doesn't get the work done or do anything good for the relationship. The scenario would need to be much worse to even consider E a viable option.

Choice C has some significant benefits even if it isn't exactly what you'd say. This type of response (not a reaction) makes the point that he went too far and provides the alternative to meeting in the morning. If he is as committed as he has implied, he should do that. You've let him know by saying "This time I'm going to pretend I didn't hear the second part of what you said" that he should think hard before slighting your commitment to the team and suggesting you pull out. In fact, he should think hard before saying anything like this to you again. And you can calmly make that clear again later at a lunch when the project is complete. And so, C has many advantages. One is how well it follows a rule given to us by that same U.S. retailer board member who advised against using threats: "Keep your position agile. It's very important for people to think quickly when someone says something offensive so you don't lock yourself in. You have to leave yourself some room, keep your position agile while you find out where they're coming from."

Sure, the critical colleague might counter Choice C with another offensive remark like the one he already made, but C limits his options somewhat. If he were to do that, he'd be escalating the altercation and doing damage to his work relationship with you and also to the project. He'd be violating the rule of reciprocal generosity. So, in many ways C is the best option.

Now that we've looked at some criteria to consider in responding on your feet with comebacks, let's look at some common scenarios at work: people spoiling for an argument, picking at your faults, trying to place the blame on you, and dangling you on a string. As we present them, think about how you would respond to each of these types. This will continue to give you a sense of what your response tendencies are and in doing so will help you determine how best to make use of the advice presented in this book.

THE SPOILER FOR AN ARGUMENT

Some people love an argument. And I'm not talking here about an intellectual debate. They want to put you on the spot, demonstrate their superiority, and, above all else, win. You've likely met people like this, as it's difficult to go through life without having done so. Just the sight of this type of person raises your blood pressure. Unless, of course, you either spoil for an argument yourself on a regular basis, you are a glutton for punishment or, better, you are prepared with what to say.

It's useful to know how to manage spoilers since they are an inevitability in life. One way is to frustrate them with agreement. *"I see what you mean"* and *"I hadn't thought of it that way"* are two phrases that decline altercation. They give away nothing, but are likely to diminish the spoiler's power to make you miserable.

The additional advantage is that few things bother someone spoiling for an argument as much as the other person being agreeable (especially when they're actually not agreeing at all). It's masterful really and a good technique to have in your toolbox of comebacks.

Another comeback option is using the spoiler's own words to support your ideas. You listen to what the spoiler has to say, and then put a twist on it, such as agreeing with part of what he says as support for what you're proposing. In the conversational example below, the spoiler's success is circumvented by using his words to support a way of proceeding that is different from what he is advocating:

"This isn't going to work. Forget it. We've tried it before."

"Not recently, though."

"This project is too important to take risks with failed ideas."

"Precisely. And that's why we're better off tweaking something that almost worked, an idea that came from a lot of smart people at this table, than going off half-cocked trying something totally new."

The best spoiler is one that hasn't read this book or considered these options and so doesn't realize that he is being managed. He underestimates you, and so you can come out unscathed.

Suppose a colleague says to you, *"I talked with Tim and he is not happy. He mentioned your part in the project's failure. It doesn't look good."* You have a lot of choices here. Among them are:

Alteration

"I talked with him too and he was in a much better mood by then. But thanks for the heads-up."

No disagreement in the above, but it alters an aspect of what the other person said in order to draw a different conclusion—in this case, concerning time and mood change.

Reinterpretation

"We both know Tim is too smart not to realize that failure often precedes phenomenal success."

Again there is no disagreement directly with the argument. This time the premise regarding Tim's mood is not addressed directly. Here, the idea that Tim's mood suggests he's looking for someone to blame is rejected. This is achieved by stepping aside from disagreement and by complimenting Tim's ability to benefit from experience. At the very least, this leaves the spoiler confused. After all, you haven't challenged him or her.

Both of these responses so far are especially useful if your goal is to return the relationship to a positive one and if the comment that provoked your response is neither highly insulting nor substantially negative in intent.

General Observation

"Some days are clearly better than others, and the good news is that I know that" (said as you walk away).

Here again there isn't direct disagreement but rather an analysis of the situation that supersedes the one proposed—in this case applying to a general rule about life's good and bad days. It avoids confrontation.

Context Alteration

"If I were the only person he mentioned regarding the project, maybe I'd worry."

Refusing to be pulled into negativity or to become defensive by finding something missing in the other person's description of the situation is often useful. Here, pointing out that other people were mentioned in Tim's comments weakens the validity of the claim that Tim considers you (alone) to be the reason for failure.

Intention Revision

"Thanks for the tip. You're always watching my back."

This is diversionary and turns the focus back onto the speaker and does so (to the extent you choose) in a slightly sarcastic way. When done well, this throws the spoiler off course by refusing to interpret his obviously negative intentions in the way he wants.

There's also a general dismissal of intention and meaning. Here you don't address what is being said but rather treat it as a "blip" in life.

Moving On

"What I want to know is: What's for lunch?"

Moving on can be a useful option, especially if it causes the spoiler to reflect upon what she said or to learn not to try using her special negativity skills around you.

THE CRITIC

One of America's most famous artists, Norman Rockwell, was criticized for being a mere illustrator instead of an artist. One analysis, published in the *New York Times* in 1999, questioned the basis for Rockwell's high status among artists, professors, and critics:

> *Rockwell's covers for* The Saturday Evening Post . . . *transport you to a small-town Eden untouched by avarice or crime, a place where everyone says grace before dinner and ends the day in front of a hearth. When you look beneath the surface in Rockwell, you find more layers of surface.*[1]

What did Rockwell do about such criticism? Not the expected. Instead of arguing that he must be taken seriously as an artist, thus dignifying insults with defensiveness, Rockwell turned the tables on his critics and told them that he was pleased to be an illustrator—an achievement to which he'd always aspired. He replied:

> *To us, illustration was an ennobling profession. That's part of the reason I went into illustration. It was a profession with a great tradition, a profession I could be proud of.*[2]

This kind of reframing response to criticism is often effective. It doesn't work all of the time. But when people think they're insulting you and there is something about the insult that could be considered a compliment, why not respond calmly, accept the label as something you actually find positive, and take the wind out of the sails of a cheap shot?

There are times when a person is known for being a malicious critic and so deserves a response that gives him or her some of the same. This must have been the case when Winston Churchill famously responded to Bessie Braddock, a British labor politician, who had accosted him at a party where he'd been drinking. *"Sir, you are drunk,"* she chastised. To which Churchill is reported to have replied: *"When I wake up tomorrow I will be sober. But you, madam, will still be ugly."*

Her nickname, "Battling Bessie," gives us reason to believe that Churchill wasn't the first to be berated by Braddock. So Churchill likely believed she was inviting his response, or that it was time someone stopped Bessie in her tracks. Below are some general responses that you'll want to reserve for rare occasions when people have significantly exceeded your tolerance threshold:

"You know, when I look into your eyes, I see the back of your head."

"I liked your approach; now let's see your departure."

"You ought to do some soul searching, maybe you'll find one."[3]

Responding in these ways to significant insults, usually with a smile, is not only appropriate but also gratifying. It reduces tension and, on occasion, puts the insulter in his or her place.

Jane Austen, author of such novels as *Pride and Prejudice*, *Persuasion*, and *Sense and Sensibility*, was often criticized for focusing her work on the middle class—her own class—and virtually ignoring the lower classes and the aristocracy. And although she lived during the time of the French Revolution and the Napoleonic Wars, these were often said to not have impacted her work. But Joan Rees, author of *Jane Austen: Woman and Writer*, refers to Austen's knowledge of her limitations as one of her greatest strengths. Rees explained: "In the course of her reading, she had recognized constantly the absurdity of writing on any subject imperfectly comprehended."[4] Here again, as with Rockwell, something considered a weakness can also be regarded—and was by Austen—as a considerable strength.

This is a very important technique to master. And it's important to remember: if you listen well enough to what is being said in criticism or an argument, within it is almost always something that you can agree with, or emphasize as the real issue (to your advantage), or turn into a positive merely by viewing it from a *different vantage point*—as the Stewart-Ray example demonstrated in chapter 2.

A New York attorney with a list of clients most lawyers would surely envy counts this line among his favorite comebacks: "I won't say you're wrong about that. But let's look at your statement from a different angle." He explains: "Conflict-resolution geniuses don't have plans. They are totally willing to listen, find out who wants what and what is being argued about. They say, in one way or another, 'I'm not sure why you said that, so I'd like to know the reasoning behind it.' They don't establish a vantage point from which to view what is going on until they've gathered sufficient information. And then you might hear them say, 'Here's what I think is going on here' or 'Here is what Jason thinks is going on here,' bringing the insulter into the creation of a shared vantage point that works well for as many people involved as possible."

Along with excellent listening, a little education can also be a good thing in terms of formulating responses. If you're well read, for example, you have the advantage of being able to place a caustic remark within a historical context, thus rendering it uninformed. Rockwell might have reminded his critics that Michelangelo's work on the ceiling of the Sistine Chapel in Rome can be seen as illustration. And indeed it has been by many art experts.

THE BLAMER

This type is everywhere, especially in highly political workplaces and wherever jobs or promotions have become scarce. People spend a lot of time trying not to look as if they caused failures. One way to achieve that is to point the finger of blame at others.

Ted Turner, founder of CNN and former owner of the Atlanta Braves, was faced with the blame for the team's bad fortunes. And in his memoir, *Call Me Ted*, he admits that over the years, the leadership had done a pretty poor job of running the ball club. That would change, but in 1983 Turner faced considerable team losses. He received a call from Rankin Smith, then the owner of Atlanta's football team, the Falcons, who said, albeit in a friendly way, "Ted, I have to ask you. What does it feel like to lose a hundred games in one season?" Turner replied, "Well, I don't look at it that way, Rankin. The way I see it we won sixty-two games, and that's more than the Falcons have won in the last ten years!"[5]

People who try to blame others and embarrass them are often people who underestimate those they're attacking. This is a good thing if you're the one being attacked. It leaves them open to the kind of response Turner offered. It may have been all in good fun between him and Rankin, but the same kind of comeback—turning the tables—can be used with less appreciated aquaintances as well.

One of the most difficult things to do in communication is to refrain from attacking when being attacked. Think of it, rather, as being suckered into a fight that will distract you from your goals. That usually helps. Of course, there are times to fight back. And sometimes you just have to take the wind out of someone's sails or they're going to sink your boat. But often it's better to say one of the following to at least buy you some time:

"There's plenty of blame to go around on this one."

"We can spend an hour pointing fingers or we can turn this around."

"Blaming other people doesn't fix the problem."

"We could make this personal, but I don't see the point."

THE PUPPETEER

People who lord power over others, especially those who do so for their own pleasure or ego gratification, are able to do so largely because they're good at discovering what matters to people and are allowed by those same people to stand between them and those goals or desires. In short: most of us at some time in our lives allow people to make us anxious or miserable because we have failed to strip them of undeserved power.

At her Ph.D. graduation celebration a family friend told me about a professor who'd been on her committee all during her dissertation development. Each time she visited with him, he said, "I'm sure it's all fine" and sent her off believing anything she produced would please him. Two months before she was to defend her dissertation before the faculty of her Ivy League college, this professor said to her, "Wait a minute here. I have to read everything you've done from the beginning. I don't know if you're ready to defend your dissertation. Give me all the work you've done at every step."

Imagine how you would have felt. She had only weeks to go, and the committee member she'd worried least about was now holding her hostage. She went through a few days of terror, but then decided if this is how he was going to be, she'd go along, confidently giving him what he'd requested. She could have rightly accused him of academic negligence. She might have argued with him about the appropriateness of his sudden interest in her work and accused him of purposely waiting until just before her defense so he would have power over her and her advisor. All of this may have indeed been true, and she would have been well within her rights to mount such a challenge. Instead, she decided that all of this could wait. The first road to take was the one that acknowledged his importance by giving him all that he'd requested. She believes that having chosen not to fight him actually made him less interested in blocking her graduation. So all worked out for her. Sometimes the best way to deal with power like this is to wait to challenge it until absolutely necessary, and to not appear rattled because this is exactly what some people hope to achieve. As the sage advice goes: "If you show them your Achilles' heel, they will surely kick it"—another way of saying "Never let them see you sweat."

In this case, the path of least resistance, as long as she could keep it open and still achieve her goals, was the best strategy. Had he started to lord his power over her simply to be a big shot, then she would have had to challenge him. Keeping it from becoming personal would then have been useful, especially early on. She might have said,

> "I asked you to be on my committee to learn from you. Given where we are and the time I have left before the defense, what do you recommend?"

The compliment provides a context for her request. It compliments while also indicating her intention to stay on schedule. He might have said,

> "The flaw is too serious. You'll need to postpone your dissertation defense."

She then would have needed to assess the degree of support available from her other committee members. Assuming he was the only one concerned, the only one seeing a "fatal flaw," she could have said,

"I can address this in the time we have. I'll work with you as often as you like."

This response requires him to devote his time to fixing the problem. It is not too much for a student to ask. And if his purpose were merely to lord power over her and other committee members, his unwillingness to devote considerable time would reveal that. He would look unprofessional.

I remember consulting for a law firm in which a division manager would always throw a monkey wrench into the works. He'd find a problem just before a final decision, and it would frustratingly send them back to the beginning. When he did this while I was present, I suggested that since he was perceptive enough to identify the problem, he should be the one to fix it. I outlined a number of steps involved, including the time-consuming work he could do. He withdrew his objections and miraculously the problem disappeared.

Whenever someone tries to be an obstacle out of habit or power needs, try giving him or her extra work to address the problem. They won't continue being an obstacle for long.

THE COMPLAINER

We all complain. But some people take it to extremes. You see them coming down the hall and you know they're going to make you feel bad or annoy you. So what do you do? If you're 75 percent responsible for how people communicate with you, then surely there must be a way to deal with this situation constructively.

You could tell the complainer about Will Bowen, a preacher in Kansas City, Missouri, who gave his congregation bracelets to remind them not to complain. He thought complaining was getting out of hand and that it was not good for people. The bracelet had the word

"Spirit" on it. He asked members of his congregation not to complain for twenty-one days. Each time they complained, they were to take the bracelet off and put it on the opposite wrist. Then they were to begin their twenty-one days of not complaining all over again.[6]

Bowen believes that negative words lead to negative thoughts, and that negative thoughts produce negative results. Of course, being stoic isn't always the best way to handle life's tougher moments. But if being negative becomes a habit, it usually needs some tweaking.

Cognitive behavioral therapists sometimes use "thought stopping" to help patients replace negative thoughts with positive ones. And that's a good way to make sure you don't become a complainer. It's useful for getting yourself in a better mood, or for being able to segment problems into one part of a day, perhaps after work and with friends, so you can focus on your job during the rest of the day.

So, do you tell a constant complainer about this technique? You could. It depends on the circumstances. Or, you might complain in return after the complainer stops talking and then say,

"Look at us. We're being those people who bring themselves down by complaining. Talk about things negatively, I read, and it affects your thoughts and what you do. I'm heading out to get a soda to cheer me up. Want one?"

Or how about—

"My technique for dealing with these things is to replace a negative thought with a positive one. Try it."

Of course, if this person's situation is quite serious, that response is insensitive. You have to judge whether he or she is a complainer by nature or if this situation is different and a little understanding is necessary.

If he or she is constantly complaining and you don't want to be drawn into listening to a negative diatribe, here are a few more useful comebacks:

Nod, close your eyes, and sigh empathically. Then—

"I don't dwell on such things anymore. You shouldn't, either."

"There are peaks and valleys and level plains. I'm working on level today."

"There's a positive slant on that, too. We both have jobs."

"I only allow myself to complain for five minutes each day and my time is up."

"I only entertain negative thoughts for five minutes, and I'm over my limit."

"We should try looking on the bright side when we see each other tomorrow."

"You can let them get to you. But are they worth it?"

"Can't do complaining today. Did it yesterday and it didn't help."

"If they know they're getting to you like this, they've won."

"I'm going back to my office. I'll meet you here in two minutes to start over on a more positive note. It's healthier."

"At times, being here can be like being deprived of sunlight. But I've learned to limit the effects. You should, too."

THE "IT CAN'T BE DONE" TYPE

I can't tell you how many times I've coached people dealing with "the system" and some bureaucrat who has spent a career memorizing manuals and contorting rules to suit their company's purposes. They want to treat most complaints in the same way: by distancing themselves and the organization from blame and making you feel as though you just didn't follow procedure or stay within the supposedly clear rules in some manual no one, besides people like themselves, even knows exists.

So what do you do? Well, it isn't foolproof, but you attempt to pull the human being out of the bureaucrat. I may know what you're thinking: The ones I know aren't human anymore. But often that isn't the case. They're trying to keep their jobs and they're willing to do some unsavory things at times to accomplish that, but many are human underneath. If you don't access that part of them, or at least try, you'll merely be the recipient of a laundry list of ways you caused your own problem.

You could say something like this:

> "Bill, surely you know me well enough to talk to me about more than a list of rules. Tell me how other people have dealt with this. You have that expertise. I don't."

If you know the person even reasonably well, another approach is possible:

> "How many years have we known each other, Bill? It must be at least ten. So let me ask you this: What would you tell your wife [son/daughter/sister] to do if they were in my position?"

Now, some it-can't-be-done types will resist your attempts to pull them off their dry path of rules and regulations. But even these people can often be reached and valuable information gleaned. In a more personal sense, I remember when I was only about nineteen and my college dormitory became a pit of nastiness. I needed to move but couldn't afford to live off-campus like my other friends, so a transfer to another dorm was necessary. The bureaucrat in the housing office, however, refused to allow me to move. I approached my advisor and told him the story. His first reaction was, *"You have to learn to deal with people like this. And fight back."* I explained that I'd done that for months and it was taking a toll. He resisted again. So, I said, *"When Jennifer, sixteen years from now, is facing something like this in her college dormitory, will you tell her to grow up?"* He looked at me and studied my eyes, all the time thinking of his little girl, then three, living alongside the sort of destructive and distracting behavior I had reported. He picked up the phone and I was transferred that week to a great dorm. Making something personal for someone can lead him or her to an empathic conclusion. Even bureaucrats and bosses have kids, wives, sisters, brothers, or mothers for whom they would not tolerate what they'll allow others to go through because of some clause in a book. You have to tap into that.

I've also learned to hang up and call again if I get someone on the phone in customer service whose attitude indicates that he isn't going to be helpful. Who needs the hassle? For example, I recently watched a postal clerk grump at a lady as I waited in line. He coughed without covering his mouth and lectured her on wrapping boxes. When my turn came, I walked past this man to the woman working next to him. Beside her was a small sign that read: IT DOESN'T HURT TO SMILE. Sounded good to me. The postal clerk who'd just belittled the customer in front of me called to me, *"Come over here."* I turned and said, *"No thanks, I'm going to her."* He replied angrily, *"I can do whatever she does."* I shook my head and said, *"No you can't."* His face was beet red. He turned to the next poor person in line and shouted, *"You come to me."* And he did. Why? Because most people take the bureaucrat they're stuck with. But that isn't necessary.

I figure life is too short to deal with people like this. Besides, I'm the customer. He may have a uniform, but he doesn't have to flaunt it. That's how you have to handle people at work sometimes. If they're an obstacle to your goals, go around them. Why waste your time unnecessarily. Rarely is any one person the only one with whom you can work to achieve a goal.

One other particularly illustrative it-can't-be-done experience occurred when a learning resources director, for some reason, kept telling me *"No"* in response to my requests for very easily provided educational help for one of my students. She was like a brick wall— on everything. Extra supervised time for this student to finish tests was even too much to ask. I'd never met her before and people from her division sitting around her didn't seem to agree with her, even though she kept looking at them and saying, *"We don't do that."* They looked away. Maybe one nodded. So, I pushed back my chair and said, *"Something isn't right here. I don't know what it is. But I know it's a factor. Some of these requests are minor, the sort given in a heartbeat to any student needing assistance. So, what is going on?"* She resisted in an ultrabureaucratic way for a few seconds. Then she finally relented: *"Yes,"* she said. *"We've been told we have to cut back—that we have to be more consistent and not go outside the rules by adjusting to individual student needs."* I nodded and said, *"So, while I've been pulling at you to give this student the help he needs, you've been pulling back, not because you don't care about him, but because you've been told to refrain from providing services."* She nodded. *"We care very much about the student,"* she assured me, the rigid bureaucrat less visible now. *"But our hands our tied."* Now, believe me, I wish she'd said that earlier, but at least we got at what was really going on. So we agreed to reconvene when her supervisor could be there—perhaps a person who possessed the authority to give the student what he needed to succeed.

This example demonstrates that often a person with whom you're dealing is answering to other people or a set of organizational rules—of which you're not aware. Usually there are ways around these once you've identified them, but you have to be talking to the right person. Next time you find yourself talking to someone who is acting like a brick wall, consider that some background forces may be at work. Until you know what they are, you only contribute to the problem by proceeding to argue. Usually when you acquire knowledge of what is going on behind the scenes, you can find avenues for getting what you need. But not if you just keep pounding on the brick wall.

In this chapter we've looked at types of comeback challenges all of us face. Now we're ready to delve deeper and look at some other conversational ways to turn difficult situations into ones that work in your favor. Specifically, we'll look at other obstacles that stand in the way of superb comebacks. These aren't obstacles inherent in the situation but dysfunctional habits of communication that can be changed.

CHAPTER FOUR

The Perils of Patterns

In an article entitled "Good Communication That Blocks Learning," Harvard professor Chris Argyris argues that we develop mental models early in life that we later use for dealing with emotional or threatening issues at work. This, Argyris explains, can be problematic:

> One of the puzzling things about these mental models is that when the issues we face are embarrassing or threatening, the master programs we actually use are rarely the ones we think we use. Each of us has what I call an "espoused theory of action" based on principles and precepts that fit our intellectual backgrounds and commitments. But most of us have quite a different "theory-in-use" to which we resort in moments of stress. And very few of us are aware of the contradictions between the two. In short, most of us are consistently inconsistent in the way we act.[1]

If you don't understand the "master programs" you employ to construct your communication and, to make matters more complex, the extent to which you act in ways inconsistent with those in moments of stress, improving communication is difficult if not impossible. Add to this the tendency in organizations to insist that employees "suck it up" when things go awry, to "keep your own counsel," and to "not wear your heart on your sleeve," among a host of other defensive routines, it's a wonder any of us knows what's going on day to day. We are awash in deception—our own and those of the organizations in which we work.

So we start this section with a focus on individual patterns that often prove dysfunctional, along with ways to replace them with more effective forms of communication.

AVOIDING COMMUNICATION RUTS

Utah-based management consultant Valerie Whitmore shared with me her efforts to assist a promising candidate for CEO of a major electronics firm in recognizing his style limitations. Primary among these was the commanding leadership style he'd inherited from the prior CEO, his mentor. It no longer suited the organization, and moreover it was not a natural style for him. He was going against the grain, so to speak, on two fronts. Only by realizing that he was a significant part of the reason why people were resisting his promotion to CEO did he become at least 75 percent responsible for the outcome. He was inadvertently blocking the promotion with his commitment to a style that was no longer desired or functional. He was stuck in a rut, and people were ready for something different from a CEO.

Once made aware of how this rut was undermining his chances of becoming CEO, he welcomed learning about ways to change. Whitmore advised him to start with three words he'd rarely used in the past with people at work: *"Help me understand."* She suggested he approach differences of opinion with others using those three words in place of his tendency to direct all communications toward what he viewed as the right solution. He gave it a try. Initially there was the expected tendency to slip back into the commanding pattern, to tell more than ask, to talk more than listen, but in a short period of time he was able to make himself ask for information so he might better understand disparate views and to patiently listen and learn. Within a month, people were beginning to say with appreciation, "He's really changed." Many still wondered, though, if the change would stick.

After a few more months, he'd convinced everyone that he had indeed changed for good—and he had. It wasn't only the three words but also the attitudes and actions he developed along with them. "He adopted the 'help-me-understand' framework," Whitmore explained. "He got it, so to speak, and ran with it." He added new ways of saying *"Help me understand,"* such as *"Give me your thoughts on this," "Tell me more,"* and *"Why do you think that's the case?"* He soon realized that having more information helped him make better decisions. People were pleased. And he became CEO.

To this day, when he detects confrontation or resistance, rather than slip into a commanding mode, he easily moves into one of inquiry. This is an impressive and all too rare story of how individual communication patterns that don't work can be changed.

I've also coached many women over the years whose communication habits stood in the way of their success. They would go into meetings and try to make their thoughts known but would find themselves being interrupted or ignored—something that research has shown happens more often to women than to men at work. The women I've worked with simply didn't know how to regain the floor once they had lost it, or how to deal with someone who'd lifted their ideas right before their eyes.[2]

We also all know people who, when not understood, merely raise their voices as if their colleagues are deaf. Others become verbally abusive or, with a sigh of disdain, simply refuse to say more, or sputter, *"I can't talk to you."* If you're one of these people, you have your work cut out for you, because you're in a communication rut.

In these cases, the first step toward change is to admit that all of us develop patterns of interacting with others that are functional for our purposes and ones that are dysfunctional as well. What you want is far more of the former than the latter. This is especially the case for developing comeback skill. Most of the people I've worked with who haven't been effective comeback users were held back by communication patterns that were within their power to change.

UNWANTED REPETITIVE EPISODES

Much of my study of communication has focused on patterns. The upside of patterns is that we can use them in various similar situations without having to learn them afresh. Also, we can detect them in the conversational choices of others. And, as mentioned earlier, when people make themselves predictable it is easier to manage conversations with them.

The downside is that while patterns make others predictable, they make us so as well. People who fall into patterns, especially ones keeping them from learning and changing, are sitting ducks at work. So you have to be alert to what my colleagues and I at the University of Massachusetts referred to as undesired or unwanted repetitive episodes (URPs).[3] Recognizing when you're in an unwanted repetitive episode is the first step in changing the way you interact with people to bring about more favorable outcomes. My dissertation work was on how people handle, at young ages, deviations from expected events in conversation. If we learn how to handle such violations of expectations early on in our lives, it can be very useful. But many of us don't learn to do this, and we pay for it until we learn what to do when something unexpected and unwanted happens in conversation.[4]

We reinforce URPs by doing things that allow them to continue.

For example, if you're the forgiving type, it may be that people aren't walking all over you because you're often in the wrong place at the wrong time but rather because you let them. If someone exceeds your threshold of courtesy or good taste and you don't in some way apprise him or her of your displeasure, they're sure to do it again. In the next few sections, we'll explore some common examples of these URPs. Consider each case and ask yourself whether it applies to you and your workplace.

Unwillingly Divulging Personal Information

Take nosy people, for instance. Connie Kelly, board member for one of the largest U.S retail organizations, told me about some of her husband's old friends, ones she hardly knew, who came to visit their home. They stayed for the weekend. During the visit the man continuously asked personal questions such as: "How much money do you make?" "Do you both own this house or is it in one of your names only?" and "Exactly how old are you?" These are just a few of the impertinences this man engaged in throughout the ill-begotten, onerous weekend. What do you do when someone acts like this in your home? The people are visiting for a weekend. You're the host. Your spouse likes them. It's awkward at best as you feel some obligation to provide them with a good time. But clearly this man has stepped outside the bounds of propriety. What do you do? Much the same as what you'd do at work if your boss invited someone with no manners to have lunch with you. One option is to say with a smile or a slight laugh, *"I'm not sure I know you well enough to answer that kind of personal question."* Another option is to say, *"It's sometimes a limitation, but I'm a very private person."*

There are also these:

"You seem very interested in things I rarely speak about."

"Most of the things you might find interesting about me are already on the Internet, so just Google my name."

"There isn't much that's private in the world anymore, is there?"

"I have a rule about personal questions—I never answer them."

These are more risky than the earlier ones if your goal is to avoid offense. But recall that this person has not simply asked one personal question but quite a few. Someone needs to stop him. And since you're the one under investigation by this man, the job falls to you. Why let your blood pressure rise to a dangerous level simply to avoid letting him know that he has gone too far?

Some people might argue, "It's one thing to do this in my home and quite another at work." And, to some extent, that might be true. At work you may decide to use one of the less risky comebacks. But there are times, and I speak from experience, when someone grilling you or demeaning you (or both) has exceeded the threshold of acceptable interaction to the extent that your credibility is on the line. If you sit there and take it from this social Neanderthal, people with whom you work are going to lose respect for you. It's much better to find a way to stop such people. One less risky approach is to turn the tables on them. Since one of the major rules of communication discussed earlier is reciprocity, once someone asks you a personal question or two, you have every right to ask them at least one.

By reminding the offending party and anyone listening that you've already been asked personal questions, you are also reminding them that you are within your rights, as a communicator in most cultures, to do the same in return. Here's how that is done:

"Now I have a question for you . . ."

"I'd be interested in knowing the same about you. How much money do *you* make?"

"Now that we know me so well, let's focus on you."

By contrast, my friend Connie answered most of the questions posed to her by her husband's guest. By the end of the visit, she was tired and angry. "Why do I need to be nice to people like this?" she asked me. Yes, it's natural to give guests more leeway, but this guest also abused the privilege of being a guest. So she didn't have to be as nice as she'd been. She could have said:

"Since we're obviously saying and asking whatever crosses our minds, I'd like to say how much I hate this topic."

It's abrupt. But someone who is truly, repeatedly, and purposefully invading your space needs to be brought up short. And that applies at work as well. Another option would be:

"Someone needs to change the direction of this conversation, and it clearly isn't going to be you. So let me just put us on another track."

If you can't imagine yourself saying something like this because you don't have that kind of edge to your public persona, you might try one of these comebacks, which are a bit kinder:

"I'm going to let what you just said season a bit before responding."

"Do we know each other well enough to have this discussion?"

"Isn't the night a bit young for us to be getting so personal?"

During seminars I've conducted on comebacks, some people cringe or laugh at response options like these. "I can't say any of those," they insist. "They're just too abrupt for me." But think about what you're telling the person who has invaded your privacy. When you meekly answer their questions, you are indirectly saying, *"Keep prying into my private life. I don't mind."* And so they do. You've abdicated your 75 percent of responsibility. And that is never good. You can purposely decide to answer one very personal question and then say something like:

> "That's your quota of personal questions for the year"

> "Don't take my answer to that question as a signal to ask me another one like it."

> "Consider yourself special, as I rarely answer such personal questions."

If the person is not a clod, he or she should get the point. If he or she is a clod, then it's time for one of the more direct comebacks, or perhaps you could create an excuse to leave the room and see if that gets his or her attention.

Jumping to Judgment

Another common URP is a tendency to reply too quickly and defensively before determining if harm was intended. This is as dysfunctional as allowing someone to put you in an embarrassing position with personal questions. As a rule, it's best to observe a situation for several minutes. In order to become proficient at using comebacks in difficult situations, you have to know your tendencies and learn when to self-correct. One way is to simply let someone bothering you know that you normally would leap to judgment, but that this time you're doing her a favor. You might say,

> "I usually respond defensively to comments like that even if no offense was intended. So give me a moment."

It's direct, but it also gives the other person a chance to assess if indeed she intended to cause offense. Another option:

> "If I didn't know you, I'd think you were prying [insulting me, being a wise guy, trying to trip me up, making me look bad to your advantage]."

Giving people a chance to see what they've uttered from another vantage point is a kind of gift. It may not be one they seek or even deserve, but giving it can alter the course of a conversation that is about to go decidedly downhill. *Giving someone a chance to do the right thing* is what I call this strategy. Most people will take you up on the offer and alter the way they're communicating.

Giving people a chance to do the right thing can also be much more than a social gift. It can be advantageous at work. If you take the whole of what you know about a person, you may decide that on balance he is not so bad. You may think that something just said was offensive but that his past record negates (or at least mitigates) its effects—something we often do for friends. Most of us have a friend who is brazen at times, a person who when we invite him to be with our more civilized friends at a gathering is likely to offend at least one of them. But we tell others that he is really a good person and ask them to give him a pass.

There is something to be said for this. After all, comebacks are not supposed to be ways of slapping down someone we've met for the first time. Yes, that may be called for now and then, but not often. Usually we have at least some knowledge of the person who is evoking a comeback, and often we have a relationship with him or her. We often need to take that into consideration at work because our goals there are usually long term. We'll need to work with these people in the future, and some of them actually are, on balance, not that bad.

Former secretary of state Madeleine Albright was an expert at deciding who should or shouldn't be challenged verbally. A case in point was Senator Edmund Muskie. Few people got along well with Senator Muskie in 1958 when he hired the young Albright to run his fund-raising campaign. She managed Muskie by managing her responses to him. She was so good at it that he made her his chief legislative assistant in 1976—a big step up for a woman at a time when only a handful of women held senior staff positions in the Senate and there were no women senators. Muskie celebrated her appointment at a staff meeting the next day with words that would have made other women turn and leave. "At last we'll have some sex in this office," Muskie said. It was crass, funny to some, and certainly not the compliment Albright deserved, but she stuck. She knew the good and not so good sides of Ed Muskie and realized working for him was a privilege, if sometimes also a nightmare.[5]

Now, I'm not suggesting that today (or even then) women should take a comment like this without a comeback. Those were different times and women often found themselves smiling at jokes about their gender. I've rarely met a woman who was working then who doesn't have a story like this. But when you're standing in front of a large assembly of people and someone known to say indelicate things does so about you, the best response is often to smile slightly (perhaps looking up) as if you can't believe this person could be so rude, or to point a finger of warning at the offender instead of taking him on then and there. It's a judgment call. There are no perfect answers. But were that same thing to happen today, Albright wouldn't need to say much, since Muskie's comment would be seen as totally inappropriate. She could simply tilt her head and widen her eyes in warning or disbelief and that would take care of that. Again, a lot depends on the context and the times.

Behind the scenes Albright often let people know how she expected to be treated. Leon Billings, who put in three decades of loyal service to Muskie, described Madeleine Albright's skill this way: "She handled the senator as well as anyone I knew. She had clearly made a decision that she was not going to be intimidated by him."[6]

Michael Dobbs, author of *Madeleine Albright: A Twentieth-Century Odyssey*, wrote of the woman who would one day be secretary of state: "Madeleine was tough enough to put up with his fits of anger, while being feminine enough to appeal to his old-fashioned, gentlemanly side. She says Muskie's rages were usually directed at things that bothered him, rather than at individual aides." According to Dobbs, Albright said, "He yelled a lot, but he never yelled at me."[7]

Being able to separate out when someone is attacking you personally and when they're attacking an issue and you happen to be in the room, or too close by to avoid some fallout, is a rare and special skill. Albright focused on what she and Muskie had in common. At the time, her job was to help him look good. And despite his history of angry outbreaks, at his funeral she described him as her political role model, a person without whom she would never have accomplished what she did. When she became secretary of state, she placed his portrait on the wall immediately outside of her office. She learned a lot from him by focusing more on what they shared than on how they differed. Dobbs describes her talent for overlooking quirks and personality flaws in pursuit of important goals in this way:

While Madeleine's personality is obviously very different from Muskie's, they had certain things in common, beginning with an immigrant's faith in America as a shining beacon for the rest of the world. Like him, however, she is a compromiser at heart, will-

ing to make a deal with her worst enemy in the interest of getting
something accomplished.[8]

Madeleine Albright has what one of her friends described as "superior social intelligence." She knew what people wanted from her and factored that into how she dealt with them. She knew, too, how to be furious beneath a surface of warmth and charm. Without social intelligence and the ability to manage emotions and thoughts that threaten to derail us from our goals, comebacks are like a box of shiny, sharp tools in the hands of someone lacking the training and experience to use them effectively. No one develops this skill without knowing how to listen and observe.

A BIT OF ARISTOTELIAN COMEBACK WISDOM

I've found this passage from Aristotle useful when attempting to determine if an offensive comment calls for a strong comeback—one capable of preventing URPs. Often the wisdom of the ages is very useful in the present despite our tendency to treat philosophy as something old and irrelevant. As you can see from Aristotle's thoughts below, that's hardly the case. His wording is a bit complex, but what he says is worth study. He splits hairs, so to speak, in explaining "grades of misconduct"—ways to judge people's actions. And it is this splitting of hairs in deciding whether to respond intensely or to let something pass that often makes all the difference in the future of relationships at work.

Some of our voluntary acts we do from choice, and some we do
not; those which are the result of deliberation are chosen, and those
which are not the result of deliberation are not chosen. Thus in asso-

ciations there are three kinds of injury. Those that are done in igno-rance are Mistakes — when the patient or the act or the instrument or the effect was different from what the agent supposed, because he either did not mean to hit anyone, or not with that missile, or not that person, or not with that effect; but the result was different from what he expected (e.g., he only meant to give the other a prick, not a wound), or the person or the missile was different. When the injury occurs contrary to reasonable expectation it is a Misad-venture; but when it occurs not contrary to reasonable expectation but without malicious intent it is a mistake (for the agent makes a mistake when the origin of the responsibility lies in himself; when it lies outside him his act is a misadventure). When the agent acts knowingly but without premeditation it is an Injury; such are all acts due to temper or any other of the unavoidable and natural feel-ings to which human beings are liable. For those who commit these injuries and mistakes are doing wrong, and their acts are injuries; but this does not of itself make them unjust or wicked men, because the harm that they did was not due to malice; it is when a man does a wrong on purpose that he is unjust and wicked.[9]

I love the inclusion of "misadventures" as incidents where the injury is contrary to reasonable expectation. Wouldn't you like to be able to say after saying the wrong thing, "Oh, sorry. I just had a verbal misadventure." Now, that would cause people to pause. And you could do it. But that word rarely enters our vocabulary these days, especially with regard to communication, even though it provides a useful category.

Think about it: misadventures of this sort happen daily. Someone says something he thinks is harmless only to have it be received as an insult. Perhaps he slipped verbally and used the wrong word. His mouth moved more quickly than his brain.

Sometimes a person is simply tired, or has just dealt with a contentious issue and is, for the moment, seeing all others in a similar vein, or is in a bad mood, or has for some reason slipped into a bad habit. That is why it is useful, as a rule, to give people the benefit of the doubt or to endeavor to do so. Doing this sometimes involves waiting a moment before saying something like one of the following:

"Is there something I said or did that I've neglected to notice?"
"Are you angry at me, or just angry?"
"Is it me or is there tension between us at the moment?"
"There seems to be more going on here than meets the eye."
"I suggest we step back a moment, as something just went awry."
"For two people who get along famously, we're off course today."
"I may have misspoken."
"We could quibble over small stuff, or we can find a way to fix this."
"This issue is an obstacle, but not unlike countless ones we've overcome before."
"I now see where you're going with that idea. It's a good one."
"How will we deal with x if we do what you're suggesting?"
"Tell me more. That's more your area of expertise than mine."
"What if we do this part your way and the other mine and see where it takes us?"

If none of these suits you, it might work to look up in the air as if thinking, smile slightly, and say, somewhat bemused,

"To borrow from Aristotle, I think we just had a misadventure."

Confronting and Demurring Too Quickly

Unwillingly revealing too much and jumping to judgment often occur because we don't know how to stop ourselves. We slip up, as just discussed, and say the wrong thing before we have a chance to think. The same thing happens when we go for the jugular or demurely walk away in response to what we see as an affront.

You can actually identify whether you tend to confront or avoid asserting yourself by labeling the kinds of comments you make. Confronting comments can be labeled one-up (⇑) moves in communication. If you demur or somehow acquiesce to the other person, it is one-down (⇓). There is nothing inherently wrong with either of these types of comments. But if you're doing one or the other too often, or at the wrong times, it can be costly to your career and other relationships. The short conversation below shows how this can happen.[10]

Ashley: The next time you want to correct me in a meeting, think twice. (⇑)
Lois: Did I do that? (⇓)
Ashley: You do it all the time. (⇑)
Lois: I didn't mean to offend you.(⇓)
Ashley: I don't care what you meant to do. Just don't do it anymore. (⇑)
Lois: It won't happen again. Sorry. (⇓)
Ashley: It'd better not. (⇑)

I've written about this type of directionality labeling before, but in terms of comebacks, the consistent use of either one-up comments or one-down comments can lead to problematic patterns. As we've discussed, doing so makes you predictable—and people can use that to manage you.

A good remedy for this is to insert more one-across (⇒) comments in what you say, especially with people who tend to evoke from you too many one-up or one-down reactions. One-across comments are particularly useful in generating comebacks because they give you a chance to think. The best communicators use them to buy some time and to avoid being predictable.

Silence is often a one-across move. But as a comeback it is not for everyone, nor does it serve on most occasions. It can be perceived as losing an argument or as rude. Also, it's difficult sometimes to manage our nonverbal reactions. So, you might try another option that also buys time for you to think, while also giving the other person a chance to reconsider what he or she said. A colleague of mine described with amusement someone who, when perturbed by something said to him, would often reply, "Now, could you just run that logic by me again?" In the course of trying to "run the logic" the other person would usually reconsider what he or she said and rephrase it to be more positive.

When someone says something offensive, in place of silence you might try one of these: *"I see,"* *"That's interesting,"* *"Hmmm,"* or *"I hadn't really thought of it that way."* None of these counters or concedes. They are not one-up ($\Uparrow$), such as *"You're totally wrong,"* or one-down ($\Downarrow$), such as *"Was I really that bad?"* but noncommittal and hence one-across ($\Rightarrow$). If not said sarcastically, one-across utterances can be very effective ways to reroute a conversation that isn't going in a constructive direction.

Now that you know about URPs, you can also say in the middle of what appears to be an accelerating argument or standoff, "I could be wrong, but we seem to be in an URP." This will bring the conversation to a halt for sure. If the other person hasn't read about URPs, he or she will need to ask what you meant by that comment. That's when you might engage in what communication experts call "metacommunicating," or communicating about your communication. "We seem to have gotten into a debate mode when we both intended to have a discussion" is metacommunication. I've tried this quite often and it works well, especially if indeed a dysfunctional pattern has emerged in a conversation. When they ask, "What's a URP?" I usually say, "We're in an unwanted repetitive episode and I think there's a way out." Usually the person is quite interested. My students and people I've coached and trained have tried this, too, and most reported back that it not only worked like a charm but was fun in the process. They tell people when asked about URPs, "I learned about them in class and I think it's happening here" or "I read about them recently and I believe we're in one." Most people are then curious.

An additional benefit of this metacommunication strategy is that it allows the dysfunctional direction of the conversation to not be the fault of any one person but of a pattern. Once this pattern is discussed, it's possible to suggest another route. You could also simply say, "I think we're in a pattern." But the term "URP" is more likely to generate a pause in conversation and curiosity.

Returning to the conversation between Ashley and Lois, the latter could have replied to Ashley's initial assertion with "I have to say I'm surprised." Responding like this is not an aggressive attack and it isn't acquiescent either. It's in between. This kind of approach keeps the door open to discussion about what occurred. Instead, Lois took the blame and kept it throughout the conversation, perhaps for something she didn't even intend to do and may not have done by any standard other than the one Ashley adopted.

Using one-across comments is a much underutilized comeback strategy. Most of us move quickly either to take over or give in during conversations. We employ far too few one-across moves and in this way get suckered into traps in conversation. Why not try one of these instead:

KEY ONE-ACROSS MOVES TO REMEMBER

"Tell me more."

"Run that by me again, would you?"

"That's a twist I hadn't considered."

"Another way of saying that would be . . . ?"

"That's intriguing."

"I'm going to take a moment here to be sure I understood."

"Let's slow things down a bit."

"There are a couple of ways to take that."

"I'll pass on my turn; you keep talking."

"My goodness."

"Really?"

"You don't say."

"I see."

"Uh-huh."

"Is that right?"

"Humph. That's something to think about."

"That's a lot to take in."

"I'm wondering if I heard you right."

"I'm sensing a caution light here."

"I get your drift."

"That's a point to consider, for sure."

"A lot of people would choose silence right now."

"I like to reflect on comments like that one."

"Now, I wonder. Should I take that as an insult or a compliment?"

Of course, some of these would sound sarcastic if not said in a way meant only to buy time. Nevertheless, even at the risk of being taken the wrong way, these comments and ones like them can redirect a conversation away from a downward spiral.

There is much to be said for learning how to utilize one-across moves, if for no other reason than to give you a chance to pause, collect yourself, and choose the response you really want to use.

If you're deficient in this area, try starting with "*Hmm*" next time someone says something that puzzles you or puts you on the spot. If that doesn't suit the situation, try one of the other "Key One-Across Moves to Remember" outlined above. See how it goes. See if the person reconsiders his or her approach or asks you what's on your mind, thus bringing their chain of one-up control moves to a halt. It's a small thing to do but can have significant effects, especially if people are used to you always defending yourself right away, taking control, or giving in. If you practice, you'll no longer be at the mercy of people who see you coming, who know exactly what you'll say or do, because you have in your repertoire some novel comebacks that just might leave them, instead of you, at a loss for words.

In the end, URPs are communication patterns that keep us from thinking creatively. Instead, we slip into old patterns and deprive ourselves of opportunities to alter the course of conversations and relationships if we don't identify and manage them properly. In the next chapter, we'll look at what happens when we don't even get a chance to fall into URPs.

Specifically, we'll explore that "frozen in place" feeling that so many people get when being put on the spot keeps them from making confident comebacks. We've all been there, and it's frustrating at best. By the end of the next chapter, you'll have a much better sense of how to rid yourself of that reaction—and become more confident in the process.

CHAPTER FIVE

Overcoming Comeback Brain Freeze

One of the most common frustrations that people express to me is their inability to respond effectively on the spot. Like URPs, this is a habit, but it's a breakable one. You just have to get at the root of why it keeps happening. Is it lack of confidence, or are you missing a toolbox of comebacks waiting for the right situation? Maybe you had some bad experiences early on, or maybe your family wasn't good at comeback versatility, so you're not either. There is something to be said for families passing on communication wisdom, but if we're at least 75 percent responsible for how people treat us, we can't be always blaming our parents. That's an all-too-easy out. We need to take charge. And so, in this chapter we're going to lock horns with brain freeze. Once we've done that, between freeing yourself of URPs as much as possible and defrosting the comeback part of your brain, you'll be a much more skillful communicator at work.

A MIND IN SHOCK

We're social beings, and so to be excluded is painful. Most of us desire inclusion, and some of us find sufficient amounts of it with family and among friends. However, others look to work for that feeling. Work, though, is usually a competitive place, even when people get along. So, even in the best of workplaces, there will be difficult times.

It's possible to find a minimally political organization where people really like and care about each other, and I wrote about one such company, Patagonia, in *The Secret Handshake*.[1] While I found Patagonia to be a place where people came first and where concerns for each other and family were clearly evident, I've rarely found organizations like this in all my days of studying businesses, coaching, and consulting.

In most organizations there are people who want your job or simply don't like you or your ideas. And so they seek to exclude you in one of many ways. When you're on the receiving end, that usually feels bad on an emotional level. But to make matters worse, as research at UCLA shows, such exclusion can actually lead to physical pain as well. If you don't know how to protect yourself from exclusionary attempts, if your brain freezes when you try, you're not only inviting awkward and career-derailing events at work, you're opening yourself up to actual physical hurt.

Specifically, UCLA psychologists have determined for the first time that a gene linked with physical pain sensitivity is also associated with social pain sensitivity. The study indicates that variation in the mu-opioid receptor gene (OPRM1), which is often associated with physical pain, is related to how much social pain a person feels in response to social rejection.[2] People with a rare form of the gene are more sensitive to rejection and experience more brain evidence of distress in response to rejection than those with the more common form.

And as if it weren't bad enough that people need to make us feel excluded and that leads to physical pain, recent research also indicates that unlike many types of pain that we cease to remember, socially induced pain can be brought to mind long after—almost as if it's happening again in the moment. So once you've felt excluded, the resulting social and physical pain can be relived through similar circumstances.[3]

These researchers' findings raise a question each of us should ask: How sensitive am I to insult and rejection? Does it cause me psychological and even physical pain? If so, then you have even more reason to learn how to handle such situations effectively. And if indeed you do have such reactions to the way people treat you, it may also be the case that your mind shuts down in a kind of panic to protect you from further hurt. You might also respond in ways that get you out of the situation rather than in ways that are likely to prevent it from occurring in the future.

As if the linkage between social injury, physical pain, and their long-term consequences weren't enough, researchers have, as just mentioned, found that the mind can go into "shock" in the wake of social pain and essentially shut down. The same can happen in anticipation of it, too—what we're calling here "comeback brain freeze." In cases of severe physical pain, the body protects itself with a reduction in sensitivity to pain—what we often call numbness. Social exclusion can also produce an initial reaction of no emotion, a kind of freezing, or numbness, of the brain.[4]

So if you're not good at managing interactions at work, when faced with a socially challenging situation that falls under the umbrella of potential or real rejection, your ability to respond may be compromised by a socially induced brain freeze. It isn't that your brain isn't developed enough to provide an effective comeback; but some situations are so painful socially that even the most clever of us—even if we've learned many good comebacks and feel confident in their use—can be stopped in our tracks when reminded of past pain. This is as problematic an obstacle to effective comebacks as URPs.

Thus, it's important for you to do a brief analysis of past social pain to see if the extent to which you freeze when verbally accosted at work might be due to past history. I'm not suggesting that you seek therapy to find those experiences; I'm simply recommending that you open yourself up to the realization that you can think on your feet even if you now tend to mentally freeze in place when faced with a comeback moment. It's just that some early experiences may be holding you back. After all, comeback brain freeze, especially if it occurs early on in our lives, is often memorable because it's embarrassing or frustrating. And it takes only a few experiences like this to get into the brain freeze habit. Eventually you find yourself becoming frozen in place when someone says something you know deserves an astute comeback. But habits can be broken. And comeback brain freeze is no exception.

For most of us, breaking a comeback brain freeze habit requires developing an extensive repertoire of comebacks along with practice, practice, and more practice. You can't wait around to be a sitting duck when your social and physical well-being are in jeopardy, especially at the hands of someone out to get your job or simply to make you feel bad so they can feel better. If that doesn't make you want to improve, to develop your comeback repertoire, then I don't know what will. Maybe just the thought that it's always a better day when you don't go home with your "tail dragging between your legs" because some wise guy verbally flattened you and you did nothing.

This book's coauthor, Chris Noblet, remembers how he used to stutter whenever he entered the office of one of his bosses. She was quite incapable of expressing what she needed but was free with criticism. "This isn't right. I don't know what's wrong with it. You better fix it" was her typical reaction. No amount of effort to obtain specifics worked. She would just repeat, "This isn't right. It's not acceptable." She did this to everyone who worked for her. Chris explained: "She was probably just covering for herself by blaming everybody but herself. She wanted to be able to tell her boss, whom she feared, that the people who worked for her were inept. Or she just didn't know what she wanted from people. Maybe both." In any case, it made everyone working for her nervous, and several, like Chris, had physical reactions to the frustration of working for such a person and her insults. His brain would freeze and he felt trapped in an endless cycle of "produce and be insulted for it."

Ultimately, out of desperation, Chris walked into the office of his boss's supervisor and said, "I can't seem to do this correctly and I can't get the information from Leslie how to do it correctly." He didn't say anything negative about Leslie. He took the chance that her boss knew she wasn't an effective communicator. This vice president looked at the report and very clearly provided what Chris needed. After that, Chris bypassed his boss on important occasions when he needed clarification. It had the additional benefit of the vice president realizing, as Chris put it, "That I wasn't a complete idiot."

This strategy also produced one even more unexpected benefit: the vice president started to go directly to Chris with jobs. This told his boss to tread more lightly, and at the same time it opened up an avenue for Chris should things get worse. He could bypass her and try to work for her boss. But until he'd made himself 75 percent responsible for how he was being treated and did something about the physical and emotional response he was experiencing, being at work had been a living hell. Had his direct boss been approachable and willing to listen to what the people who worked for her needed, going around her wouldn't have been necessary. And certainly in most offices this tactic is frowned upon and so can backfire. But there are times when there is no choice and little to lose, because the immediate boss refuses to communicate.

Mike Prout, a senior manager with twenty-five years in the same pharmaceutical company, told me of a comeback moment he'd regretted. His boss, with whom Prout got along well, was prone to taking humor too far. Every five years Prout's company would give their people an item of their choice from a list, and Prout chose to receive a company tie tack on this particular fifth-year anniversary. On this occasion, his boss asked him to come to his office. When Prout arrived, the boss was talking with someone from office head-quarters. He motioned for Prout to sit down, then, during a pause in his phone conversation, asked him how the research was going on an important project. Prout replied, "I'm having a hard time with it." His boss didn't like that answer, especially while on the phone with someone from headquarters. He wanted to be able to report that things were going along well. He picked up a small box and threw it at Prout. "Here's your five-year anniversary gift," he said with a slight smile. But Prout knew this boss's smile didn't mean it was all a joke. "He's passive-aggressive at times," Prout told me.

Prout didn't think it was funny. He felt humiliated. An interest-ing aside is that several years earlier this boss had told Prout, "You know, Mike, you can always tell me to f— off." Instead, Prout said nothing. "I sublimated and allowed a guy who knew how to push my buttons to do it again." Prout added, "In hindsight, he learned from my lack of response that he could push, push, push and I wouldn't confront him." I asked Prout what he'd say if he had it to do over. He said, "I would have told him, 'I worked hard for the last five years and it was humiliating and degrading for you to throw the tie tack at me.'"

Prout told me he couldn't imagine himself ever saying "f— off" to his boss, even though he had been given permission. But it was still nagging at him many years later. He knew that his boss prob-ably had wanted him to say, while on the phone with someone at headquarters, that the project was going well. But Prout told him the truth. He also told me during my interview with him, "In cor-porate America, as a rule, you bite your tongue a lot." That's what he did—and he was still regretting it many years later. He'd had a brain freeze moment, a shock from having had his anniversary award thrown at him. But he could have said something hours, or even a day or two, later. He didn't, and to this day he regrets that choice.

Here is an option that Prout might have used:

"You once said I could tell you to f— off. Consider yourself told."

That's a delicious comeback, isn't it? And one tempting for most of us, even if not easy to implement. But look at it this way. It doesn't directly tell the boss to "f— off." It alerts him to having been served. It's slightly less direct, and it artfully uses the permission granted a few years before as a lead-in to the main message. So many people I've coached over the years wish they could at least once in their careers say something like that to a boss. The truth is that most comeback situations don't warrant it. But when someone throws a five-year anniversary gift at you when you've been a great employee for twenty-five years, after they've told you to tell them something specific if they ever get out of hand, the groundwork is there. But for most occasions, here are options more along the lines of Prout's style:

"You're funny sometimes, Al. But not this time."

"Next time don't use me as the butt of your jokes to please the guys upstairs."

"You're the boss, Al. But that doesn't mean anything goes."

Given that they had a good relationship, I would have been in-clined to go with a strong comeback. This was one of those times when the person richly deserved to get as good as he'd given. And even if Prout wasn't able to give back as good as he got, he could have come close. And that's what the "consider yourself told" come-back would have done.

THE PONDERING GENE

Comeback brain freeze can also come from simply being too analytical. A prolific start-up investor told me that he had to fire a CEO of a new company he backed despite her being an Ivy League graduate with impeccable credentials. Why? She thought long-term all of the time.

> *She had to go over and over reams of data every time she made a decision. She couldn't skim the stuff, get the gist, and run with it. It drove me crazy. She was simply too analytical. And with start-ups especially, you can't be pondering every decision from every angle while the competition buries you.*

If you're in the habit of thinking and gathering information for long periods of time before acting at work, you're likely pretty slow on the uptake when it comes to comebacks. Let me be clear, however: I'm not saying that effective comebacks require impulsiveness. But they do require sensitivity to the existence of a propitious moment. So you have to ask yourself if you're in the habit of reading a situation for far too long.

Whether it's fear or habit that causes brain freeze, it's important to practice getting around it. If you tend to be overanalytical and that gets in the way of employing comebacks, the next time you're facing a problem with someone, use your analytical skills to answer the following questions:

1. Is my credibility with those looking on in jeopardy?
2. If I don't respond effectively now, will this person surely feel free to do it again?
3. Is there little if any doubt that she intended to insult me?
4. Is this not the first time he's gone too far with me or others?

5. Is what she said unacceptable by nearly any standard?

If the answer is yes to several of these questions, then certainly you need to start to employ comebacks that will correct at least the worst of these. Don't worry too much about making a mistake. It's somewhat like skiing. It's better to take a fall and get up again than to worry your way all the way down the mountain. That's not even skiing. And taking potshots from someone on a regular basis isn't effective work either. So, if your brain freezes and you let people get the best of you, it's surely time to do some thawing out and letting them know, pleasantly if you prefer, that those days are over.

BYPASSING COMEBACK BRAIN FREEZE WITH METAPHORS

We didn't want to write a book that provided you with nothing more than quick one-liners and zingers. Some of the best comebacks are metaphors—images that make an impression on people, that reframe what is before them, often in graceful ways. And the beauty of metaphors is that the good ones tend to be memorable, and that serves future comeback needs. They pop into mind when a similar situation arises and not only guide behavior but also provide persuasive images to use when communicating. This quality also makes them useful in overcoming comeback brain freeze. If you have a set of metaphors in mind, then when you are stumped for what to say, you can call on one of them (e.g.: "What we need here is a long drive over the fence or the game is over"). That's why sports metaphors pop into conversation so often. If the situation seems competitive or in some other way reminds people of lessons learned through sports, then metaphors about sports easily come to mind and help them bypass brain freeze. The same can be said for other categories of metaphors heard frequently during childhood, such as those about use of time.

"Never wait for a train or a woman [or man]. Another one will come along soon" is an image I kept in my mind after learning it. If you think back, your life has at times been guided by such sayings, images, and metaphors. "A stitch in time saves nine" but "Haste makes waste" are two opposing ways to look at the use of time, just as "Absence makes the heart grow fonder" and "Out of sight, out of mind" describe contradictory ways of looking at personal relationships. Whether one or the other applies more to the situation at hand is left to the discretion of the speaker.

We *save* time and we can *waste* time. We *fall* in love but rarely hear of people *falling out* of love, though it seems feasible. People *break up* and whoever does so first often is viewed as being the one with the *upper hand* or the one who was more aggrieved. Language affects how we think, and how we think affects our language. Indeed, language is powerful and can influence us to say and do things before we have a chance to consider if it is dysfunctional, inappropriate, ignorant, or in some other negative category.

Linguist George Lakoff asserts that we actually can think in metaphors.[5] Once we appreciate an image like "the road not taken," from Robert Frost's famous poem, we can call upon it to understand a confusing or unsettling point in our own or someone else's life. To the extent that you train yourself to think in terms of metaphors, the more likely it is that you'll be able to access them when you need to break out of a bad case of brain freeze.

Metaphors—and indeed images and descriptors of any sort—can be used to insult, so it's also useful to know how to respond when they're used against you. I recall when a professor disparaged me in a graduate-level class by saying, "Kathleen, anyone can be an eclectic." He didn't like the way I was conjoining ideas from different schools of thought to find a solution to a problem, because he belonged, body and soul, to one school. The comment hurt. It was tantamount to saying, *"You're all over the place in your thinking, so you're really nowhere."* After class, I happened to pass by the office of an internationally esteemed professor of rhetoric. *"You look a bit down,"* she said to me. *"What's on your mind?"* I told her. She looked amused. *"Well,"* she said pensively, *"it's true. Anyone can be an eclectic."* I nodded. Indeed, I was all over the place—hopelessly adrift in a sea of ideas, far from land. *"But,"* she added with emphasis, *"very few can be a good one."* I looked up. She smiled broadly and added. *"And you, Kathleen, are truly a good one."* Thanks to her generous observation, backed up by that sincere smile, at that moment I came to regard myself as a rigorous eclectic, as opposed to some wishy-washy thinker.

So if a narrow-minded person tells you *"You're at sea on this one,"* you might reply, *"Beats being landlocked all your life."* If you're young and someone dismisses your contribution by laughing as he or she says, *"You're a babe in the woods,"* a useful reply might be a counter metaphor: *"I thought out of the mouths of babes come words of wisdom."* This can be very effective. It's a *touché* of sorts and if said with the right inflection and nonverbal expression—perhaps a slight smile—it can be disarming.

In my negotiation classes, I have taught students to frame their ideas with metaphors and also how to reframe the other side's metaphors to your advantage. Both are powerful techniques as often "a picture is worth a thousand words." You can take a metaphor used by the other side and expand on it to support your own view, or you can counter, as just discussed, with a better metaphor. I wish I'd saved all the good metaphoric comebacks my undergraduate, Executive M.B.A., and International M.B.A. students came up with over the years, but here's an instructive sample: One team argues, "We all have to be on board to make this work." To which the other side replies, "That'd be fine if the ship weren't sinking so fast. A sturdy lifeboat is what we're proposing today."

Metaphors appear in many other ways in the workplace, as well. For years it was nearly impossible to get through a business day, or certainly a conference, without someone talking about "thinking outside the box." It was used to elicit ideas that weren't the same old, same old. Or, as was often done, it could be used to justify a truly ridiculous idea. After all, "thinking outside the box" was a supposedly good thing—and often it was for companies stuck in ruts. But, as with many metaphors adopted by companies, after a while it came to be used for just about anything unusual, no matter how much sense an idea made or the potential for its successful implementation.

Thinking outside the box was its own justification; the metaphor had become entrenched. Challenging entrenched metaphors is not something most people do comfortably or wisely. And so, such metaphors continue to be used until finally—mercifully in some cases—their usage falls away when they are considered antiquated by those who have found another metaphor more to their liking.

The point to be made here is that while a metaphor is in good stead, it can draw many nods and cause people to categorize your ideas in positive ways. So it pays to know the metaphors in favor where you work.

"A mistake is a gift" was big during the Total Quality Management era. It meant that failures were to be valued as learning opportunities, and certainly there's a lot to be said for that. Of course, it was used as an excuse for some pretty big mistakes rather than as the opportunity to take responsibility and learn from mistakes.

"Paradigm shift" had a good run as well. Thomas Kuhn coined this term in his very influential 1962 book *The Structure of Scientific Revolutions*, and it was intended to describe for the hard sciences a change in a fundamental model of events. When abnormalities are noted that cannot be explained by the current, universally accepted ways of thinking, scientists begin to challenge that current paradigm. If the anomalies can be explained away by error or by some other acceptable reason, the paradigm remains intact. If more and more anomalies are found, however, science experiences a crisis and a paradigm shift may occur.

And who, of course, does not know about the "tipping point," the level at which the momentum for change becomes unstoppable? After Malcolm Gladwell's book *The Tipping Point: How Little Things Can Make a Big Difference*[6] became a best seller, few did not know the term. It was used in business and continues to be used today to describe that point at which change is inevitable. People no longer need to say things like, "Soon we'll reach a point where so much will have happened to move this along that there will be no stopping the change to come." Reference to a "tipping point" suffices.

Metaphors are also particularly important in the workplace because they can separate the in-group from the out-group at work, even when those metaphors aren't used for that purpose. Would you know what was meant if someone at work said, "Let's call an audible"? For those of you who don't know, this is a football term. When the quarterback, after eyeing how the defense is arranging itself, changes the play on the fly, he's "calling an audible." So if a product is tanking in the market, someone might say, "Let's call an audible and drop the price."[7] Imagine dropping that line into a conversation as a comeback. In most places it would certainly bring the conversation to a halt. In others it would be just the thing to say, the kind of expression that causes everyone in the know to nod. If you don't understand the term, though, it can often lead to not knowing what to say next.

Is it any wonder, then, that often those most astute at comebacks are also those capable of crafting or calling upon compelling metaphors? With just a few words they can make actions that seem inexplicable suddenly appear to make sense. Whether used for good or not, to condemn or to justify, effective metaphors "grab" us, influence our thinking, and stick with us; so it pays to know which ones work well where you work and to have a few new ones up your sleeve—just in case you find yourself at a loss for words.

BYPASSING COMEBACK BRAIN FREEZE
WITH A REPERTOIRE AND PRACTICE

Bypassing the brain freeze that results from fear or habit is a matter of rerouting, retraining the brain to see such situations as opportunities or challenges—whichever gets you moving—as opposed to entrapment. This is important to remember. It's crucial to building and utilizing a comeback repertoire. It's freeing, too. Once you see that social brain freeze is a chemical reaction or a matter of habit, you don't have to treat it as an inevitable aspect of your personality. Think how meditation can slow your heart rate, and how exercise can make you more fit for most of life's ups and downs. Training the mind to see a potential workplace disaster coming your way, and learning how to prevent or deal with it, is no different. Think of a firefighter who knows how to get up a ladder to save a life. He or she doesn't do that without a lot of learning and practice. That's exactly what you need if you want to learn to bypass social brain freeze.

Here is a set of comebacks you might want to keep tucked away to help get you past brain freeze. If memorized, they can get you over a rough spot until you decide what more to say.

BRAIN FREEZE BYPASS COMEBACKS

"Is that the best you've got?" (before moving on)

"I see you're pulling out all the stops here—using your best stuff."

"Were you making a point or simply trying to amuse yourself at my expense?"

"If I seem perplexed, that's because I'm thinking about giving you the benefit of the doubt."

"If you think that was funny, you need a new gig."

"I'm going to step over here and pretend this didn't happen. Care to join me?"

"There are times when silence is the only option. This is one of them."

"I'm not sure that you really said what I heard you say."

"Give me a moment while I reconstruct what you just said into something tolerable [more enlightened, civilized, intelligent, perceptive, sensitive, etc.]."

"My brain is on pause at the moment, which is serving both of us quite nicely."

"Let me just say how little I have to say in response to that."

"Of all the things I thought you might say, that was certainly not one of them." (Or, "Of all the things I knew you might say, that was certainly one of them," letting this person know how predictable he is.)

"If I said what I'm thinking, we'd both be out of line."

"I've known you too long to believe you intended to insult me."

"*I* know—you restate what you just said, and I won't say what I just thought."

"I could use some help interpreting what you just said."

"I'm sure you won't mind waiting while I give more thought to what I'm about to say than you just did."

"This seems a good time to take a break—to reflect on what we're trying to achieve."

Add some of your own to these. And take a few to work over the next week or so and try them out. Unless put to work, comebacks don't stick with us. It's like studying a foreign language and never using it. So with each of the chapters here, try what we've discussed and then keep using it. In time, you'll have a repertoire of comebacks and rarely experience brain freeze again.

CHAPTER SIX

Choosing a *Relevant* Comeback

We've discussed how comebacks work, what gets in the way of employing them effectively, and how to bypass or overcome those obstacles. This chapter is the first of three that will help you choose and use the comebacks suited to most of the situations you face at work. It's fine to learn a list of comebacks and try them out, but it isn't the best way to go about becoming good at using them. You have to make sure the ones you use suit the conditions at hand.

Right now we'll provide you with a short-cut method for getting started with choosing and using relevant comebacks. We'll look at ten categories of comebacks to keep in mind—or just to keep at hand as a list in your desk. If you use the latter approach, the professor in me advises you to take that list out and review it now and then, so you will be prepared the next time you need to respond "on your feet." Even if you deal with that situation later in the day, or the next day, or in an e-mail, refer to the list for help.

You'll also find in this chapter a chart that will help you decide when to employ intense comebacks and how to gauge the degree to which positive versus negative comebacks are suited to a variety of situations.

THE COMEBACK R-LIST

I've always marveled at how effectively some scientists have rendered statistics an impenetrable mystery for most people. But while it may be a challenge to learn statistical methods, as with most forms of knowledge, the more you study the more proficient you become. And usually there are shortcuts or mental mnemonics that can assist you to learn, especially if the subject at hand doesn't come easily to you.

I had a great chemistry teacher in high school, Tracy Smith, who took the fear out of learning chemistry for me and infused it with joy. Surely you remember a teacher who did that for you in some subject or other. Teachers and professors who make subjects too difficult to learn may be protecting their intellectual turf, but they're doing little to help their students learn. Let's skip that route. There are few subjects, if any, that if presented in an organized manner can't be learned by most of us.

Comebacks are no different. It needn't be a mystery how they operate, and their effective use isn't reserved for an elite group. Now, if you're already quite skilled at thinking of comebacks, then you might decide to skip this part. Then again, however, it may serve you as a useful review or a way to organize what you already know. After all, anyone can become more skilled at comebacks. Start by learning to use the "Comeback R-List" below and you're well on your way to significant comeback improvement. Here's the list, and then we'll go into each technique in more depth and discuss the types of situations in which they are most effective:

The Comeback R-List

Reframe: Cast the issue in a different light. (*"This isn't a fight, it's just a disagreement."*)

Rephrase: say it in a different way that works better for you. (*"Another way you could say that without getting my back up is . . ."*)

Rejoin: disarm the other person with an offhand phrase or witty retort. (*"Whatever spins your wheels works for me."*)

Revisit: use an earlier success to redefine a current failure. (*"We've always worked well together. Let's not change course now."*)

Restate: clarify or redirect. (*"So what you're really saying is that we disagree on this one issue?"*)

Request: ask a question. (*"Can you tell me more about what you just said? I may be misreading something here."*)

Rebalance: adjust their power over you. (*"As it turns out, I won't be needing your help on this problem."*)

Reorganize: prioritize the issues to your favor. (*"Your third point is actually the most important. Let's start there."*)

Rebuke: chastise them; bring them up short. (*"If that was meant to be funny, you missed the mark."*)

Retaliate: get back at them. (*"Since incivility is your style, I have a few choice words for you as well."*)

There are many other forms of comebacks, some of which we've already introduced, but this list is a handy tool to help you think more quickly and to call up various types of comebacks that can work for you, without having to reread this book over and over. Now let's go over each of the "R"s with an eye toward examining when and where they work best.

REFRAME

We're starting with this for a good reason: it's one of our absolute favorites. As you'll recall, we discussed in chapter 1 how people inadvertently or purposefully use words that define other people or situations in ways that don't encourage positive outcomes. Keep in mind that words are often weak vehicles for accurately conveying what you mean and words that may seem similar actually can mean quite different things.

Here's an example. "Mary admits there were other ways to handle the situation" conveys quite a different meaning from the sentence, "Mary agrees there were other ways to handle the situation." The word "admits" can strongly imply to those hearing it that Mary was somehow wrong, at fault, or bull-headed, and that she now reluctantly acknowledges that realization. The word "agrees," when substituted for "admits," produces a markedly different meaning. Mary may be a pleasant, cooperative sort of person; or perhaps she has thought things over and wisely changed her mind. We can interpret this sentence to mean that Mary bears no fault in whatever occurred but has come across new information or has always understood that there are other ways to deal with the situation. People hearing the first sentence, even if they know that it isn't quite accurate, may well let the inaccuracy pass through their accuracy filter. If you're Mary, and you let the first meaning stand, that's not likely to be good for you.

As you likely recall from high school English class, words often have both denotative (i.e., dictionary) and connotative (i.e., commonly used, or implied) meanings. To say "Why are you shouting at me?" implies that the other person is being angry and aggressive.

We may avoid creating that frame, and the defensiveness it's likely to cause, by saying instead, "Why are you raising your voice?" Both sentences accurately describe the situation in dictionary terms, but the second one doesn't imply anger and aggressiveness (on the part of the person who's speaking so loudly) to nearly the same degree as the first. Can you see how the second response frames the shouter's behavior in a way that is more likely to cool off, defuse, or salvage the situation?

Thus, reframing as a comeback strategy involves *taking the words used by the other person and altering one or more of them to change the denotative and/or connotative meanings in order to direct the interaction toward your desired outcome.* Look at the conversation below to see how easily this can be done, if you're paying attention to how the words used by the other person threaten either your goals or how other people perceive your actions.

Peter: What were you thinking in that meeting?

Ted: What do you mean?

Peter: You were making them angry. Couldn't you tell?

Ted: I had their attention if that's what you mean.

Peter: Had their attention? They were foaming at the mouth.

Ted: That white stuff was teeth. By the end they were smiling.

Peter: But the path you took to get there was treacherous. You could have ruined your career in there.

Ted: Peter, no one pays attention to a coward. They'll no longer forget who I am, so I think today may mark a new beginning for my career here.

You can see that Ted took every one of Peter's negative assertions and altered it to become a positive one. He could have replied to "You were making them angry. Couldn't you tell?" with *I was not. You're just afraid of your own shadow.*" Ted took Peter's description as merely one person's opinion and replaced it with the more positive observation of having gotten attention rather than fading into the woodwork. Ted didn't react defensively to his colleague's barbed comments, even though they invited it as an option. He reframed by using different words to describe the same event. Then, instead of denying that it may have looked like the other people at the meeting were angry, Ted redefined the "foaming at the mouth" as smiling white teeth, evidence of pleasure and approval. He finished by arguing that the meeting could have been a " new beginning for my career" (rather than its end, as Peter suggested), and he assured Peter that it's better to be seen and heard than to be ignored as a coward.

Framing is a marvelous tool, and practice in its use is crucial to becoming skilled at comebacks. So the next time someone describes you or one of your actions to your disfavor, try revising what he's said in a way that enables a more positive view to emerge. If you only improve by making use of just this one skill, you'll be far ahead of the many, many people who allow the words that others use to dictate the prevailing perspective. You'll rarely find it necessary to become angry when people use words that detract from your accomplishments—because you'll be able to rephrase their words to your advantage and thus increase your power to create or negotiate a better outcome.

REPHRASE

Rephrasing is a close cousin to reframing, but it's not so much about changing meanings as it is about making sure that the words someone has used were accurate. It's about fixing slips of the tongue by other people that, if left unaddressed, could send an interaction or relationship down a dysfunctional path.

Rephrasing often begins with, *"If you meant to say . . ."* or *"I think a better word for that is . . ."* or *"Did you mean to say . . . ?"* It requires a pause in conversation, a moment of stepping back from what has been said, in order to help the other person say what you believe they intended but failed to actually express.

People quite often use the wrong words to describe things because they're speaking quickly, or they aren't thinking about how their words might give the wrong impression, or both. Rephrasing works well with the strategy we looked at earlier of "giving the person an opportunity to do the right thing." Let's say that something has been said that is incorrect or offensive—but you believe the person speaking did not really intend to create an uncomfortable situation. Then you help him or her get the words right, so that the conversation can move in a positive way.

Here is how rephrasing works:

Agatha: Your embellishment was a good way to change things.
Fran: You know, if you use that term it might be taken to mean that I tried to make things look better than they are. We both know you didn't mean that. Why don't we say I just clarified things a bit.

Some people might not take "embellishment" to suggest slight deception, but certainly it can be taken that way, and Fran considered that a risk. Perhaps she didn't want Agatha to accidently label her as someone who makes things look better than they are, which essentially is lying. She offered a more objective word, "clarification," in order to dispose of a meaning she found unappealing.

REJOIN

There are times when people make mistakes and you don't want to call them on it. At other times, someone may say something far-fetched, and rather than correct her, you want to say something that brings her up short. In such cases a short rejoinder of the "good for you" variety can be useful. "Go for it!" and "Whatever . . ." are two more rejoinders that can avoid expressing defensiveness while letting the other person know you aren't entirely pleased. Others include:

"Whatever makes you happy!"

"If that floats your boat."

"Be my guest."

"I see there's no stopping you."

"You're a crafty fellow for sure."

These often work well when saying something more might make you look bad. Such phrases will help keep you from getting sucked into an argument or a conversation that's going nowhere. "I'll just leave you to it" and "I see you're on a roll" are two more. I'm sure you can think of others that will work well to defuse a precarious situation or to bring a strange one to a close.

REVISIT

Skilled negotiators use this type of comeback to reverse a downhill spiral. In the course of a very good conversation, sometimes just one wrong word or look can set things on a bad course. If the persons involved have had positive experiences together in the past, it can pay to revisit those in order to bring things back to a good place. Here's how this works:

Ellen: Let's pick up where we left off yesterday.

Shane: That's fine.

Ellen: So far, we've agreed on what to do about three of the four issues we're dealing with here.

Shane: The fourth one is very important to me. I won't be able to be as generous on it. So don't expect much give on my end.

Ellen: Since we've worked really well together on all the issues we've solved so far, I'd say a good foundation has been laid for finding a way forward on this fourth one as well.

Shane: Let's see if we can make that work.

Ellen might have taken Shane's warning and his comment about having been generous as mildly confrontational, but she didn't. Instead, she used their past success to bypass his negativity and establish a basis for them upon which to move in a positive way. By revisiting their earlier success, Ellen built the case that despite Shane's concerns, success in the future can be expected as well. Since work conversations can easily go off course when people show signs of stubbornness, this comeback strategy is useful to keep in mind.

Just when you feel inclined to react to someone's negativity, try to put the encounter on a better course by reminding this person that you two (or your departments, companies, etc.) have succeeded together in the past. It doesn't need to be as broad in scope as Ellen and Shane have experienced with three out of four issues already being decided cooperatively. Even if there's only been one time—perhaps even within the current meeting—when things went well, or when the person now threatening to halt the progress actually co-operated or facilitated progress, revisiting it can be used as an anchor for the remainder of the interaction.

Here are a couple of examples of how that can work:

"Five minutes ago, Sam, we were humming along. You were leading us to what looked like terrific progress. It'd be a shame to lose that now."

"Excuse me, but are you the same person who had me practically eating out of your hand three minutes ago?"

It's always useful to watch and listen for points in conversation and negotiations when the tone starts to take a turn for the worse. At such times, revisiting a moment when things were better and linking that experience to the present can be a wonderful tool.

RESTATE

Given that we're all at least 75 percent responsible for how we're treated, we must accept that there will be times when we elicit offensive or insulting remarks from someone by virtue of what we've just said or done. We may create a misunderstanding by using words or ideas that aren't appropriate to the situation or that are expressed in ways that offend the persons with whom we're speaking. It's easy to do this. We've all done it. The key is not to react to their retaliation as if it makes sense.

When you say or imply something that you wish you could take back, take it back. You've no doubt done this in the past. Here are some ways of restating what's been said in order to put an interaction back on track:

"Hold on there. I must have said something the wrong way."

"Let me back up a bit, because I didn't intend to make you angry."

"You know, if I had that to say over I surely would."

"Was that me who just said that?"

"Did I put my foot in my mouth yet again?"

"Oh . . . I see what happened here. It's my evil twin again."

If you do this well, people can be quite understanding because, after all, they've been in such situations themselves. Of course, using any of these too frequently can actually cause people to become less tolerant of your gaffs. They have a right to expect you to improve after you've recognized your own occasion of speaking before thinking or "running off at the mouth" without consideration of who you might be offending. You don't want them to think of it as a personal tendency of yours. That caveat aside, there are a host of ways to use restatement to help a derailed conversation get back on track.

Even when it's not your fault—or at least not entirely—you may want to graciously assume more than your share of responsibility and say, for example,

"I may have said something incorrectly just then."

"I can see by your expression that I didn't quite say what I meant."

"I'd been meaning to say something complimentary and somehow it didn't come across that way."

"Can we take this conversation back to where it was before I derailed it?"

What we're talking about here is a willingness to take slightly more responsibility for conversational derailment than might be accurate. Why? Because the other person is so busy getting upset that he can't be objective. You're the one who said what's placed him in this state, so you might actually *be* responsible to a large extent. Even if he shouldn't have taken your expression or what you said the way he did, you probably could have expressed yourself more effectively. And so why not admit that, if it helps keep the conversation from going down an unproductive path?

It's another story, however, if this person is always taking things the wrong way. If that's the case, then in order to work effectively together, the two of you will need to get at why it keeps happening. It may have little to do with what you say and more with how he sees you. Does he view you as a know-it-all or think you're always bossing him around? Did you say something a long time ago that still makes him angry? Do you remind him of a fellow student he disliked in elementary school, or a teacher who flunked him? Who knows? In order to find out, you'll probably have to ask. In such circumstances, it won't pay to keep taking the lion's share of responsibility when things go wrong in conversation. You'll need to get to the root of the problem, perhaps over lunch or even with a mediator, and work from there.

In other cases, though, when something has gone wrong in the conversation and the person is occupied with wrath, disdain, or feelings of hurt, you may have to be the one who gets things back on track. This is one of those places where people who think they're right most of the time—as well as those who lack a full awareness of how easily words that were meant to convey one thing are interpreted as quite another—experience difficulty. "If I'm right, why should I do his work for him?" they ask when I'm coaching them. "If she can't listen, I'm not going to bother talking with her!" and "It's tough in this place, so I can't be going around soft-pedaling everything just so he can *feel* good!" are other protests of this type.

Here's what I say to such people: "I understand what you're saying. And it may even be accurate. But you work with this person and something is clearly wrong. You can be right or you can be effective. It's your choice. Besides, we're not talking about coddling somebody forever. We're talking about breaking a pattern or saving an important conversation when it goes awry. Personally, I'd go with making things work better, and you have the skills to make it happen. She doesn't. You have the ability to teach her what you know about how easily communication can go in the wrong direction. And that kind of objective approach to what's been going wrong can save a relationship."

REQUEST

Despite the fact that far too few people employ this comeback type, it is so important that it may even deserve a chapter of its own. Right next to Reframing, and perhaps in front of it, you should put Request at the top of your list. Post this message in your office or put it in your desk drawer, where you'll see it regularly:

WHEN IN DOUBT, ASK!

We don't ask questions often enough. Even today, in many workplaces questions are often seen as signs of poor listening skills or of weakness. After all, don't true leaders already have all the answers? They don't, and most of them will readily tell you that. While I was director of the Sample Presidential Fellows Program at the

University of Southern California, I had the privilege of working with Warren Bennis, director of the Leadership Institute and a true expert on the topic. Take a look at Warren's work as well as that of the people he cites. You'll see that the leader who has all the answers simply doesn't exist. It's a fantasy. The most effective leaders are inquisitive; they want to learn what they don't yet know before taking significant actions.

When you are in doubt about why a person said something or reacted as she did, just request more information. Check your perceptions. Gather some data. Don't shoot from the hip. However, that can be difficult to avoid in a fast-paced corporate culture. When I discussed our tendency to react impulsively in the workplace with the West Coast investor I introduced earlier, she simply responded, "That's how we do things, isn't it?" She was describing the reality, but also talking to me about learning how to request more information and find more effective ways to talk to those people who don't deliver what she wants. "It's our culture. Isn't it? I mean I never learned in business school to ask many questions. If they're not doing their jobs or say something stupid, they get slapped and usually fired."

Of course, she doesn't physically slap people. She does so verbally. And she doesn't hesitate to fire people not living up to her expectations. She is very direct and attributes much of her success to that characteristic. Keep in mind, however, that she doesn't work daily in an office with people who report to her or who work with her on multiple projects as team members. Much of her work is accomplished on the telephone or at occasional gatherings of coinvestors. Also, she needs to move quickly, deciding which new ventures to back before others step in ahead of her. Nevertheless, she still thought it would be useful to have other ways to deal with people, instead of always being the tough guy she'd learned to be in order to do business in the highly charged, competitive markets in which she works. I suggested, as I have to many people who now communicate more effectively, that she learn to become a master of inquiry. She's gotten much better at it, which has paid off in terms of knowing whether to take a financial risk on an emerging company. And her questions aren't only financial ones. "What do you think of the CEO," she'll ask. "I mean your gut instinct. Does he know his stuff? Is he motivated and committed?"

Unfortunately, questions tend to be shunted off to the "soft side" of doing business instead of being at the forefront, where they belong. In my experience, they should always be front and center in negotiations, as well as in any contentious interactions between people. Keep in mind that smart, capable people ask questions. They have inquiring minds and don't act without trying to obtain adequate information. The same applies to those who are astute users of comebacks.

While it takes a confident person to use questions in businesses where doing so might be misconstrued as indecisive, it's often the wisest move. The good news is that there are ways of asking questions that don't imply indecisiveness or lack of knowledge.

Suppose someone says to you, "You're a pain in the neck." A natural reaction would be to get annoyed or even angry. Instead, you might try asking, *"As compared to what?"* The next time someone snaps at you, why not ask: *"Is this a passing mood or should I come back tomorrow?"* If you are criticized in front of others, consider asking: *"Are you okay today?"* or *"Was that your best shot or do you have something better we can all enjoy at my expense?"* Sure, those may be a little bit sarcastic, but sometimes you have to let others know you're not a sitting duck for insults, while at the same time offering the chance to rethink and revise their approach.

Let's also focus on some of the many ways of using questions constructively to gather information without offending others, even while moving the spotlight from yourself and directing it toward the person who has attacked you. Remember the old dictum for news reporters: "who, what, when, where, why, and how" (aka, "the five W's and an H")?

Who:

"Who put that idea into your mind?"

"Who do you intend to benefit by what you're saying?"

"Who else should we bring in on this discussion?"

"Who else should know about this discussion?"

What:

"What's your real objective here?"

"What are you trying to accomplish with this line of talk?"

"What makes this line of discussion necessary at this time?"

"What are you planning to do to improve this situation?"

"What's your supporting data for these statements?"

Where:

"Where did you get your information?"

"Where should we move this discussion so that the largest possible number of people can benefit?"

"Where would you like our working relationship to go from here?"

When:

"When should we talk about this more extensively? Is this the best time?"

"Don't you agree that an issue like this requires some time to reflect? When should we discuss it again?"

"When should we be expecting to fix this? Is there a short-term solution?"

Why:

"Why are you behaving this way?"

"Why are you speaking to me in that tone?"

"Why don't we try and approach this in a more positive way?"

"Why are you bringing this up at this time?"

"Why do you think this will contribute to our productivity?"

How:

"But enough about me. How have you contributed to this situation?"

"How is this going to help us get our job done/help the company/improve our productivity?"

"How are we going to get a positive working relationship out of this?"

"How are you going to contribute to fixing this?"

"How do you think this is going to benefit your career?"

One caution: Try to follow the well-known advice given to lawyers in the courtroom: you don't want to ask questions to which you don't already have a good sense of the answers or to people whose answers you aren't prepared to respond to effectively when you get them.

Often the answers you get can be used as a basis for you to ask another question. If you haven't studied the Socratic method of using questioning to direct someone to a desired conclusion, I'd strongly advise you to do so. Socrates wasn't afraid to be wrong. In fact, scholars argue that he believed we should know the extent of our ignorance if we are to become more knowledgeable. Yet as a rule people tend to operate on unchecked assumptions. Rather than ask questions and discover what is at the base of an assertion, they simply proceed to agree or disagree with it. This is largely why so much that could get done effectively at work doesn't.

So the next time you're dealing with a difficult situation at work, or in some other aspect of your life, try asking questions that get at what is really meant by what has been said. Or just ask questions to give the other person a chance to rethink whether what he or she said was indeed what was meant.

REBALANCE

The Rebalance comeback is all about taking back power. Power consists not only of what people accrue by wealth, status, position, or force, but also of the influence we give them over us. It's certainly desirable to maintain enough power over your own work and your own life to feel that you have some amount of control over your destiny. To the extent that you can avoid being placed in situations where someone can hold up your work or make you miserable in other ways, you're maintaining (or, hopefully, improving) the balance of power in your own life. Unfortunately, though, this balance is often lost at work.

If you've read *The Secret Handshake*, *It's All Politics*, or *The Skilled Negotiator*, you already have a good sense of what I'm referring to when I say: Power is ours to take away. Many people don't think of it that way. And so they regularly end up stuck in power-imbalance situations. Instead, it's wise to carefully examine how much power we cede daily to people who don't deserve it.

If you're frustrated by having a project stalled and your time wasted, you can get angry, try to get even, or work to rearrange the situation to put yourself in charge of the outcome. In any case, the goal is to take away another person or group's power to make you miserable.

Academic administrator Sherry Price knew layoffs were imminent and that having been hired only a few years before, her job was at risk. Her work was outstanding and she had the performance appraisals to prove it, but senior executives had advised her to consider looking elsewhere, just in case. Connections, she observed, were becoming more important than competence. Price decided to generate her own visible connections. She contacted the most senior executive she knew and asked her to write a letter of recommendation to use with the people running the company. They would listen to her, Price believed, because she'd garnered considerable respect.

"Of course," the senior exec replied heartily, "we don't want you to go anywhere. We're working on keeping you here, for sure. So I'd be glad to write the letter." Three weeks passed, then four, and the letter of recommendation was still not forthcoming. The few times they passed each other in the corridor there had been friendly waves—but no mention of the letter. By the time Price spoke to me about this continued delay in obtaining a letter that was so heartily offered, she was becoming visibly upset.

"Maybe it's me," she said, "but my evaluations are terrific. Yet if she thinks that highly of me, why hasn't she written the letter? She must have decided that she doesn't want to write it.

"In any case, why such a lack of professionalism and common courtesy?" she went on. "She's not so busy that she can't let me know that she's either working on the letter or hasn't gotten to it yet because of some problem. But I hear nothing."

She was struggling not to blame herself, but the executive's rebuff caused Price to construe certain things that other colleagues said or did as more of the same. Even though she'd gotten along with coworkers, she began wondering if they were in it together.

"I can see why you're feeling that way," I said, but then I suggested to her that she deal with one slight at a time. When you ask someone to write a letter on your behalf and they drag their feet, then—no matter the reason for the delay—you need to take back some control. One way to accomplish that is to write the letter for them. Indeed, write the letter just as you hope they would write it. When you see them next in passing, tell them you know how hectic things have been and so you've put some thoughts on paper to make it easier for them to complete the letter. Let all apologies and protestations of having meant to do it sooner roll off your back. Focus instead on getting your draft of the letter into this person's hands with the suggestion they alter or add as they see fit. And close by asking, *"May I stop by your office next Tuesday or Wednesday to pick it up?"*

You can use a softer request if that's your preference: *"Would coming by to get it early next week work for you?"* If the person is a peer, you could say, *"Take a look at it and I'll be glad to come by your office tomorrow to see if you need more time."*

As I advised Price, taking positive action sure beats sitting around worrying that you've been rebuffed or dismissed, when possibly the person hasn't had a moment to think straight or may be trying to consider a better way to meet your needs. Even if she were just reluctant to write the letter (perhaps because she favors another candidate or wants time to decide whom she'll back when layoffs begin), she *did* agree to write it and so it will be difficult for her to reject your offer of help toward meeting that obligation. If you give people the control to make you miserable, to leave you hanging, often enough they will. Better to step in and make a move that gets you what you want—and, as often as possible, without stepping on toes.

Another advantage of Price doing some of the work to bring the senior executive closer to providing the letter is that, because she has given her what she needs to write it quickly, the excuse of not having time is no longer a viable reason. If she still does not provide the letter, then something else is amiss, and that's when questions, as we've just reviewed, are important. Price would need to ask if there is a reason for the delay and find ways to remove those obstacles. And if this doesn't work, it's time to find a different source of support so that power is not vested in one that continues to be nonresponsive.

REORGANIZE

This is useful when someone has prioritized issues in a way that doesn't work for you. In the midst of advancing their ideas, people usually prioritize issues whether they actually mention the word *priority* or not. Skillful communicators listen for this ordering of importance. If it gets in the way of what they wish to achieve, they'll propose another prioritization. Here are two useful phrases for reorganizing: *"Let's take these issues one at a time and start with* x *because it is the most pressing one"* and *"I see why you emphasized* y, *but it's really* x *that is causing most of the problems you mentioned. I suggest we try dealing with that first."*

Reorganizing is also useful when there is no evident order being proposed, such as when someone just provides a series of complaints, as if all of them are of equal concern. In my persuasion writing I often refer to this as "claim clutter." There is simply too much information provided to be dealt with effectively or else what is provided is haphazard, as in the conversation below between an upset Alex and his manager, Fran:

Alex: I've told Bill a hundred times that he can't go off on his own, doing whatever he wants and then implying that I've given the OK. Everyone gets confused and then nothing gets done. I'm the one who ends up looking bad, and he just slinks off somewhere and pretends it never happens. He's a loose cannon and people seem to think that's fine so long as it works. Well, it doesn't work.

Fran (Alex's manager): As I see it, Alex, Bill isn't your problem, nor is what other people think. If he does what you just described, he is the only one who looks bad. So that issue is not one you need to worry about. Let me handle that. The main challenge is making sure that people know that anything Bill tells them is not etched in stone until you have made quite clear that you sanction it. That seems to solve everything.

Fran skillfully removed from the discussion issues that she saw as irrelevant, even though Alex had given them equal prioritization with other problems on his mind. By getting him to see that Bill's behavior is a manager's problem and by taking away his concern about what others think, she was able to zero in on a solution that could resolve the primary issue of making sure people are clear about whose instructions to follow. If a communicator doesn't have this skill, his or her tendency is to simply deal with each concern raised as if all are of equal merit. That rarely solves the problem. It usually generates even more confusion. So listen to how people prioritize— or whether they do at all—and think about how to reorganize issues to address them more effectively.

Sometimes haphazard lists like the one Alex provided, as annoying as they initially seem, are actually invitations to impose order on chaos. In so doing, you take some control over the course of the interaction. This can be achieved by saying something like, *"Let's start with what you mentioned about* x *and then move to* y*"* or *"It seems to me that the issues you mentioned can be placed into three groups: those about* x, *about* y *and about* z.*"* This second approach allows the person responding to create categories that offer solution opportunities. You can imagine a manager listening to someone list concerns and then saying, *"The issues are largely ones of customer satisfaction and better team cooperation. Isn't that right?"* If the person agrees, the manager might add, *"Well, I've never known us to be incapable of addressing these types of issues effectively."*

Reorganizing is a very handy comeback strategy. *"What we have here is a failure to communicate"* is a good reorganizing comment. It creates a category for a host of problems between people. The phrase has been used so much that it might not work for you, but something like it could do the job. A couple of other examples are: *"What seem to be isolated incidences here appear to me to be largely ones of communication"* and *"If we address that, I think we'll solve most of the problems, if not all of them."* Here we're framing and reorganizing at the same time.

Useful, too, is how reorganizing is actually a focus on process. If someone presents a series of concerns along with a few personal slights, reorganizing can be used to direct the conversation away from the slights. *"You're obviously upset and rightly so. There seem to be two things at the heart of it all. If we fix those, I'd say we're most of the way home"* is an option, or you could bypass the emotions with *"I see what's happened here. And there are essentially two parts. Both are issues we've dealt with before, so there's no reason to think we can't do so now."*

REBUKE

This isn't the type of comeback that should be used liberally. It's for those occasions when directness applied appropriately will serve you best and perhaps earn you respect. If you're confident that you're clear about what the person has said, to you or about you, and that the nature of the situation (e.g., public humiliation) warrants a direct comeback, then a rebuke is an option. After all, letting people walk all over you doesn't engender admiration. Then again, neither does telling people off when you could have avoided doing so.

In order to avoid being in a position to rebuke someone, it's wise to read anticipatory clues that tell you a person may cause you trouble. Then, don't be around him or her to the extent possible. Kevin Edwards, husband of a top fashion industry executive, told us of an evening when he and his wife were out to dinner with a big client. The client had brought along some friends. One of them was a middle-aged man wearing an ascot and speaking in a fake British accent. Edwards sat beside him at dinner. As the night wore on, this man regaled him with his political views. He insisted that anyone who was even thinking of voting for the person running against his candidate was barely functioning. Edwards finally couldn't take it anymore. He'd endeavored for two hours to tolerate this man, but his pomposity exceeded Edwards's threshold when he said, "Of course FDR *ruined* the country." Edwards glared at him and shouted, "You're an idiot. I can't talk to you." Then he stood up and walked away from the table. His wife was appalled.

On the way home, Edwards's wife said, "You saw how he was dressed. You heard how he was talking. You knew what to expect. You know that people like this bother you. But you sat next to him, and just what was likely to happen did. What were you thinking?"

Those were good questions, Edwards told us. He was still angry while she was asking them, but he could have avoided the entire encounter had he read the anticipatory clues. He wouldn't have had to rebuke this man. And that certainly would have been better.

Of course, sometimes you don't have that option. A certified nursing assistant of twenty-five years—let's call her Denise Fisher—found herself working with a young man named Brent Evans, who'd recently graduated as a registered nurse. Evans quickly began acting as if he were her boss. Techniques she'd been using well for seven years he now felt obliged to instruct her in—as though she'd forget unless he told her how to do things. It was a power trip, and it was getting to her. "Who does he think he is?" she'd say to herself while driving home at night. Did this situation call for a direct rebuke? Should she have told the freshly minted RN, "Your degree doesn't hold a candle to my experience"? She worried that such a response would appear defensive.

Instead, Fisher went to see her actual supervisor. "How many bosses do I have?" she asked him. "Just me," he replied. To make sure that things were really clear, she also asked him: "So I don't need to do what Brent tells me to do?" "No," her boss confirmed. With that backup in hand, the next time Brent started telling her how to do her job, she said, "Be quiet, Brent. You're not my boss. I only have one of those and it's not you." From that day onward, Brent focused on his own job and let her do hers.

But what if she knew that one day he would likely become her supervisor? After all, he had the credentials to be promoted. Considering that possibility, if you were Denise Fisher, would you have attempted to avoid future problems by allowing him to continue telling you what to do? My take: It wouldn't work for long. If you're in an intolerable situation that diminishes your credibility and eats at you every day, why should you let your anger fester? Fisher didn't tell Evans to "Drop dead!" That *would* have been too strong. She obtained the information she needed in order to be sure of her position and then shared it with him in no uncertain terms. Few characteristics are more compelling than confidence. Once she confirmed that she was within her rights not to tolerate Evans's assumption of superiority, she dealt with the situation. Given the weeks, months, or years before Evans might be promoted—indeed it might never happen during Fisher's tenure at the hospital—there was likely enough time to get past it. All things considered, there was little need for her to tolerate a situation that was bothering her every day.

Fisher could have asked her supervisor to speak to Evans directly. That would have been a valid option, but the rebuke would not have come from her. By handling it and preparing herself, she displayed confidence, controlled the tone of the rebuke, and reduced the likelihood of commiseration between Evans and her supervisor.

Rather than offense or insult, our next example involves dealing with repeated annoyances. A medical technologist had developed a worrisome sense that a doctor with whom he worked did not trust him to do his job. He described how he used a mild rebuke to handle the situation:

> *I was covering the second and third shifts on weekends at a community hospital. We had a critically ill patient in the intensive care unit who required laboratory testing about every thirty to sixty minutes. I was performing lab testing for the entire hospital and emergency room as well as the ICU. I was quite proud that I was keeping up with the workload, but each time shortly after I returned to the laboratory after drawing a blood specimen on the ICU patient, I would receive a call from this dedicated physician asking for the test results. I understood the physician's interest and the need for rapid turnaround time, but after a while this became annoying and counterproductive. Finally, I beat the M.D. to the punch and I called him first—as soon as I returned to the laboratory with the blood specimen—and I explained that I was diligently working on his patient's testing. I assured him that I was not taking a coffee break and that the results would be available much more quickly if he would stop calling me. The calls stopped.*

Most people aren't so direct with doctors, perhaps with the exception of other doctors. This couldn't have been easy for the technologist. When you have a lot of crucial work to get done, though, and someone is creating an interruption every time you turn around, it can pay to let them know that their worries are groundless and all would go more smoothly if they simply let you do your job.

A final example of a rebuke well played was told to me by a real estate executive who expressed admiration for a female executive who was straightforward with one of her company's directors. Unhappy with recent profit performance, this board member picked her out from among the group and challenged her by saying:

"What if I cut your budget? How would you like that?"

"When you're aggressive like that," she replied, "I have to make an assumption about what's wrong. I'd appreciate you just telling me what you want."

"I talked to you that way because you're an aggressive woman," the director said.

"Yes, but no one else in the company talks like that to me," she replied. "It doesn't motivate me. So it would help for you to tell me what you want, so I can get it done."

In this case, her directness paid off. The board member respected her response. While most people in that company feared him, she showed that she was not among them—but she offered to learn from him just what it was that he wanted to accomplish. She didn't respond negatively to his comment about her being "aggressive," which certainly would have taken them off track in terms of achieving their goals. She focused squarely on finding out what he wanted to see happen.

This real estate executive was able to call his attention to how he sounded. The way she did it sure beats a knee-jerk reaction like, "Don't talk to me like that," or "Who do you think you are?" or even cowering or welling up with tears, as I've seen happen on occasion.

I coached one promising young manager out of tearing up by training her to focus on the issues instead of how the person sounded. Of course, we can all have an off day and react with anger or just fold up. With rare exceptions, though, the best way to get on track when someone is being accusatory is to steer the conversation toward attacking the issue rather than each other—occasionally that requires a firm rebuke.

RETALIATE

This one was left for last, and for a good reason. It should be used only sparingly. Yes, there will be occasions when someone "burns you," to use my son's words, so badly with what they say that you've little choice but to "burn" them back. In his lingo, "burn" means "I got you good that time." It's a victory over the other person, who is left at a loss for words.

A list of comebacks wouldn't be complete without this kind. After all, life can be tough. Work can be brutal, especially if your workplace is politically pathological,[1] but retaliation should be attempted only when dealing with truly vicious situations. After all, usually you have to work with people again. In most circumstances, there's little to be gained by scorched-earth comebacks that make that impossible. Remember the famous line "I'll see you again—on your way back down."

One memorable interview for this book involved a situation that would provoke most people to feel like retaliating. Michael Brophy has a successful career in commercial art layout and design in eastern Pennsylvania. He gives respect to and receives it from the people he works with at all levels. But when Brophy was working his way up, working conditions and employers were often tough.

One of Brophy's clients was a building supplies company where the in-house art director berated everyone who worked for her. Indeed, Brophy's advantage seemed to be that he was the only person who could stand working for her for more than a week or two at a time. As a result, he would obtain projects of a month's duration, or even longer—such as major brochures or annual reports. There was a considerable amount of stress: sleepless nights and piles of work material by the bed.

Normally, exchanges with this art director would proceed along the lines of "Michael, I made a few changes and moved a few things around. Now clean it up." These changes would usually be due the following day. He was a good, reliable performer, and she did not treat him as poorly as she did most of the people who worked with her.

One day, however, in front of at least six others, she "got right in my face about something I had done." When Brophy says "right in my face," he means it literally.

"She stuck her face no more than six inches from mine, placed her two outstretched hands on either side of her face right between us, and yelled:

"'What's *wrong* with you?' and then she repeated it even more loudly: 'What's *wrong* with you?'

"Everyone just stood there and looked at her as if to say: 'You have to be nuts to treat somebody that way.' I was shocked by it."

What would you do if you were Michael Brophy? What if someone had done this to you? Clearly she was beyond any threshold of reasonable work behavior. She humiliated him, though she did the same for herself at the time. Brophy decided that she'd done enough damage to herself. Besides, he credits his music-performance background and his dealings with all kinds of personalities in that arena with helping him develop a thick skin at work. But how could anyone just let her do this without saying something?

Brophy says his retaliation was to call in and say he wouldn't be in for a few days, and then didn't go back. He took another job offer. That's not what she wanted at all, so it was a way of getting back at her while also doing what was best for him. But what if you don't have the option of another job offer? What could you say or do in a situation like this where you work? What kind of comeback would you choose?

Here are a few possibilities:

"Do you have any idea how unprofessional you're being right now?"

"I'm going to count to two and you'd better be out of my face."

Turning to the others, "You all saw this. It's hard to believe. But you saw it."

"You'd better take some time off before you do something like this to the wrong person."

"Consider yourself lucky that I'm a patient person."

"I'll meet you upstairs in HR."

Hopefully you'll rarely if ever feel the need to "burn" vicious people in retaliation as in situations like the one above, but it's probably good to know how. Why? Think of how a well-trained black belt is able to walk calmly away from a confrontational situation that would provoke many other people. In the same way, it engenders confidence to know you *could* have said something they'd never forget but that you chose instead to go another, less aggressive, route. Brophy says that after that incident, and others, he drove home enacting what he could have said and got it out of his system that way.

It can also be amusing to think about, and share with your friends, what you could have said. Knowing you were able to control yourself in a dicey situation actually will be an indication of you how far you've progressed in your endeavors to become comeback savvy. But just in case something like this happens and it won't suffice to just walk away, consider the comeback possibilities above and others that suit your style. Let the person know that he or she had better not cross the line again. If you don't, there's little doubt that he or she will.

FINDING YOUR COMEBACK COMFORT ZONE

The comeback tactics and techniques we've just introduced, along with those in earlier chapters, may or may not suit you as an individual. So, what we'll focus on now is developing a "comeback comfort zone," and on the importance of leaving that zone only when the situation demands it. Failing to heed this rule will leave you feeling too stressed at work as a result of trying to be someone you're not.

Although an executive of my acquaintance was highly placed at an international media conglomerate, she had a boss who didn't like working with women and who let this prejudice be known. Now, this woman is no shrinking violet, so when he told her, *"You're someone who is hard to get along with,"* she could have lashed back, *"And you are an idiot!"* She didn't, though. Nor did she say, *"You're not exactly easy to work with yourself,"* or even the less personal, *"There are times when we're all like that."*

Instead, she confidently decided that he wasn't worth the effort. To respond to him in the way he deserved, she told me, would have required her to venture out of her comfort zone—and he just wasn't worth that stretch. Her reason for this conclusion: "He'll never change. So I wasn't going to waste my time trying. I put my ego out of the way, stayed away from him as much as possible, and we managed to get along."

"You have to know when to hold 'em," she quoted the song, "and know when to fold 'em."

Making these kinds of decisions are important steps in learning how to use comebacks effectively. Just because you know what you could say, doesn't mean you need to say it. If the conversation is private (as was the one above, such that your public credibility isn't on the line), and if the comment doesn't exceed your threshold of offense, then it can pay simply to stay away from the offending party as much as possible. There is another advantage here as well.

A successful senior banker told me that for many years she had enjoyed the benefits of being underestimated. "The positive side," she said, "is that people can't gear up for dealing with you. They aren't ready when you are." And that, she explained, is like having a "velvet hammer"—it packs a lot of power largely because few people see it coming.

Returning to our media executive, when another boss went even further than the first one—with an insult that was both personal and clearly sexist—she responded much differently. "I wasn't going to start trying to like him," she told me, "or even tolerate him." He'd gone well past her threshold and, while she was reluctant to share exactly what he'd said to her, it was evident from her expression that he had been way out of line. As she recounted the incidents, they clearly differed in intensity and degree of sexism. She'd let this boss know that in the future he'd better think long and hard before saying anything like that to—or even near—her.

WHICH COMEBACKS WORK FOR YOU?

As you've been reading, it's likely that you've been developing a sense of which comebacks work for you. Much like the executive above, you're beginning to develop a sense of which ones will fit in your comfort zone and which are too genteel or too aggressive. If you have a wide range, your degree of aggressiveness in terms of possible comeback tactics might look like the list below, with the least intense at the top and the most aggressive at the bottom:

- Let It Pass
  Examples: Silence or a puzzled look; "I'm letting that comment pass this time."

- Silent Eye Contact
  Examples: Pause and look into the person's eyes for a moment longer than would be expected in conversation or also shake your head a bit as if puzzled or not impressed.

- Give Them a Chance to Do the Right Thing
  Examples: "I may have misheard you or misinterpreted what you meant" or "Would you care to reword that?"

- Set Them Straight for Their Own Benefit
  Examples: "If I were you, given how things are done around here, I'd start rephrasing some of my direct comments" or "For your own good, you need to think longer before you speak."

- Consider Yourself Told
  Examples: "Be apprised that I'm insulted, and that isn't good for this relationship" or "Consider yourself told that you're a bully and I don't work with those."

- You'll Wish You Were Never Born
  Examples: Give the person a glaring look, then turn and walk away, or say something that cleverly trumps their insult or makes them look ridiculous.

These categories, with their varying degrees of intensity or aggressiveness, are meant to give you an idea of how to think about your own comfort zone. The chart below including several R-List comebacks and the more or less aggressive comeback types above may help to visualize this. Any of the entries can be moved according to what is said and how. For example, if a comment that would ordinarily be an insult is said by a friend with a broad smile on her face, the relationship and nonverbal expression would likely render it less or not at all negative. But the chart provides a visual depiction of where certain types of comments tend to be with regard to intensity and negativity.

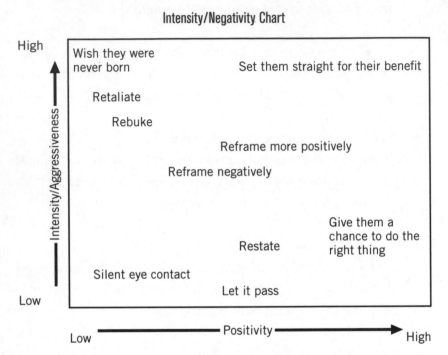

Intensity/Negativity Chart

Most of the time you will want to be able to use comebacks that stay within your comfort zone. As you brainstorm your possible comebacks for a particular occasion, try inserting them at what you estimate to be the corresponding levels of intensity/aggressiveness and positivity/negativity in the chart. Now do it again for how the other person or group is likely to receive them. Take a look at both. Then choose one or two that are clearly in your comfort zone and one or two just outside of it. If the people you'll be responding to tend to be aggressive and you're not, you may have to stretch to get their attention. Don't overdo it, though—at least not the first time. It's better to let them observe gradually that you are not as predictable as they thought.

You don't have to become someone you aren't in order to be effective at employing comebacks. However, an occasional stretch is fine—and good mental exercise—if it suits the occasion. Short of that, there's no need to be anything other than your own now more communication-savvy self.

CHAPTER SEVEN

The Gut Check

Jonah Lehrer, in his book *How We Decide*, explains that the long-accepted view that we, as humans, should strive to be more rational than emotional in our decision-making is misguided. We are both emotional and reasoning beings. To deny the importance of either is to deny a significant part of who we are and how we think.

Lehrer argues, moreover, that without emotion, reason, as we know it, would be impossible. To which I would add that being able to decide what to say when one is cornered, humiliated, frustrated, attacked, complimented, or in some other way placed on the spot, indeed requires both logic and emotion—a "gut feeling" that what you're about to say or do fits the situation at hand. This is why so many intelligent and logical people who should be able to study human interaction and do the right thing in any given situation simply aren't equipped to do so. It is also why, as Lehrer explains, the Cartesian faith in reason—a founding principle of modern philosophy that filters into the way we bring up children, how we teach them, and what we expect of them as "mature adults"—misrepresents what is needed for effective decision-making. The "gut" simply can't be dismissed. And so rather than being the out-of-control part of us, our emotions are crucial for sensing what is relevant to effective decisions.

Emotion is the companion of reason, and it is every bit its equal in determining what we do, whether we like it or not. So this chapter is about how to develop your "gut," or instincts, so that you can trust them when responding to difficult situations at work.

Carol Smith, senior vice president and chief brand officer for Elle Group, had this to say in a *New York Times* interview about gut instincts: "Every time I went against my instincts and gave a job to someone who, though clearly capable, made me feel uneasy during the interview, it has ended badly." Even when people are great on paper, she said, if they "send up little signals of alarm" it's important to take note of those.[1]

Very often it's our senses that pick up on a disconnection between what people are saying and how they are acting. Nonverbal cues, which we too often ignore in favor of trusting people's words alone, are important to determining how to proceed in any difficult situation at work.

The trouble is that gut feelings tend to be ephemeral. They can come and go quite quickly and, as a result, are often dismissed easily. After years of advising, working with, teaching, and consulting for many hundreds of successful people, no doubt remains in my mind that having and noting gut instincts is an exquisite capacity, too often underestimated by comparison with logic. But to take just one example, if we bought or rented places to live based only on logic, we'd be an unhappy lot for sure. If our cars were logical purchases alone, what fun would that be? If we were to raise our children exclusively on the logic of expert advice, never turning to our own common sense and emotional sense, how successful and satisfying would that be?

While doing research for this book, we came across an article in the *New York Times* about the U.S. military doing research on the role hunches play in early detection of dangers such as hidden bombs. To do so, researchers have conducted exhaustive interviews with experienced fighters. They have also administered personality tests and measured depth perception, vigilance, and related abilities by having troops compete to find bombs in photographs, videos, virtual-reality simulations, and mock exercises on the ground. The results of this research complements and supports other work, "suggesting that the speed with which the brain reads and interprets sensations like the feelings in one's own body and emotions in the body language of others is central to avoiding imminent threats."

Dr. Antonio Damasio, director of the Brain and Creativity Institute at the University of Southern California, describes such study results in this way: "Not long ago people thought of emotions as old stuff, as just feelings—feelings that had little to do with rational decision making, or that got in the way of it. . . . Now that position has reversed. We understand emotions as practical action programs that work to solve a problem, often before we're conscious of it. These processes are at work continually, in pilots, leaders of expeditions, parents, all of us."[2]

When we think of emotions as "practical action programs," it's easier to see why they play an important role in sensing aspects of situations that the logical part of our brains might overlook. If we're only focused on assessing the veracity of what someone says instead of how they say it, we're only getting a small part of the information we need to make good comeback choices. Our emotional selves pick up on what researchers have called peripheral information while our logical selves are busy working on central information.[3] The division of labor is not exact. The two overlap, and both are important to our getting a comprehensive sense of what is going on around us.

DEVELOPING A GUT INSTINCT

I'm often asked, "But how do I develop a gut instinct? And how do I know whether to trust it?" There are both experiential and self-confidence elements to consider here. At times in the past you've probably sensed when things weren't quite right, then gone with that sense and found that it was correct. To improve over time, you need to keep note of when that slight sense of alarm has occurred in the past and worked well for you in terms of comebacks.

Developing intuition of this sort requires attention to people and the rules that guide them. It starts with an ability to see that something a person is saying or doing is not a good fit with the situation, is perhaps overdone to please, or conflicts with small and quick non-verbal actions (or "microexpressions," as Paul Ekman refers to them)[4].

When I was a young woman one of my friends told me, "You're the most intuitive person I've ever met." I was quite flattered—momentarily that is. He then said:

But you don't listen to yourself. You know the shit is about to hit the fan before anyone else, but instead of running, you get up on a chair to see if it's really going to happen. And then—splat!

I sat for a moment, reflecting on that, thinking he was finished. Instead, he added:

But that's not all. You then pick yourself up off the floor and get back on the chair to see if it could possibly happen again.

Now, he may have been exaggerating in that last part, but I got the message. And I began the process of change then and there. Some future "splats" occurred, but fewer as time went on—at least regarding things I could sense and manage.

You might at this point ask yourself if you have a tendency to disregard your gut instincts, or perhaps to go with them too often. Either end of that range is problematic. Has a friend or someone close to you ever confided that you could do with a little less of one of these tendencies? If so, or if you've noticed one of these inclinations on your own, now is a good time to start making a change. If you're dismissive of what we call gut instinct—an uncanny sense of what is going on apart from the obvious—or if you are too quick to go with your gut instinct, begin today observing what happens when you do this. What goes through your mind? Do you sense something and then shake your head and push it out of your mind before pausing to look a little further and ask some questions? Or do you leap to conclusions based on your sense of things before taking that same kind of pause?

Now that you have in mind where you are on the range of gut-instinct reactivity, let's look at what being in touch with your "sixth sense" entails.

BECOMING A COMMUNICATION DETECTIVE

Jonah Lehrer wrote in *How We Decide* about how major league baseball players manage to hit a fastball. "The answer is that the brain begins collecting information about the pitch long before the ball leaves the pitcher's hand. As soon as the pitcher begins his wind-up, the batter automatically starts to pick up on 'anticipatory clues' that help him winnow down the list of possibilities."[5] Whether it's a torqued wrist suggesting an oncoming curve ball or an elbow angle indicating the ball will likely come right over the plate, baseball players, without even consciously studying these signs, recognize them on some level. And they act based on information less skilled ball players ignore or never see.

Olympian gold medalist Mary Lou Retton was only sixteen years old when she did her memorable "vault without fault." Retton said of this spectacular feat, "As I was doing the vault, I could feel the landing. Gymnasts have the most incredible body awareness. We can feel exactly where we are in the air." Retton could sense her landing even as she was opening up and her feet were going downward. It would be perfect.[6]

Why is this important to us? The same sense of how things are going to go occurs in conversation for those proficient at comebacks. If you're sufficiently observant over time, you pick up anticipatory cues about what a person acting in a certain way is likely to say or do next. And before you even realize it, you're getting ready to respond in some fashion that may have worked well for you in situations of this type in the past.

If you know a particular colleague well enough, you can sense in advance that he or she is about to launch a sharp-witted attack on one of your comments. In such circumstances, you can be ready. While writing this book, we were reading the novel *In the Woods*, by Tana French. The novel's protagonist, a Dublin detective named Rob Ryan, must cope daily with his irascible boss, O'Kelly, whom Ryan studies carefully in order to manage upward. French is very skilled at conveying Ryan's frequent reliance on his gut instinct. Here is one passage in which Ryan's gut kicks in before his conscious mind has time to assess what is going on:

My body understood first: I went cold all over, my breast bone tightened and it was hard to breathe. I don't know how I knew. It was obvious that I was in trouble: if O'Kelly just wants your basic chat, he sticks his head in the door, barks, "Ryan, Maddox, my office," and disappears again, to be in place behind his desk by the time you can follow. Phone summonses are reserved for when you are in for a bollocking. It could have been anything, of course . . . but I knew it wasn't.[7]

This is how gut instinct feels. You know something, but you don't know how or quite what—and your body knows first. You realize that you've been in this kind of situation before, and your mind changes from the "cognitive miser" it normally is to one that pays attention. We know on a primal level that something is either happening or about to happen. We sense that we'd better be ready.

If people weren't such creatures of pattern, the type of prediction Ryan uses to assess what's coming with his boss would be extraordinarily difficult to make. But because we are such creatures, we often reveal clues as to how we are about to proceed in interactions. And the observant communicator can become a communication detective at work by picking up on these cues before most people. Like a Green Beret or Navy SEAL, this type of communicator likely experiences a rise of stress hormones. She's alert as information pours in and she begins to formulate a response, does a quick assessment of conditions, and then proceeds to select from among learned responses or to formulate a relatively novel one. The decision process looks something like this:

Comeback Components Model

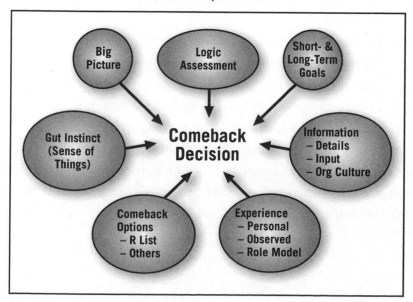

An effective comeback can come from only these three components in the comeback decision process: gut instinct, current information, and episodic memory. But people proficient at workplace
comebacks also consider their goals and those of the organization
(both long- and short-term), as well as which responses have worked
for them in the past and which haven't, and the big picture (i.e.,
what matters most on a large scale). To employ comebacks effectively at work, you need to train yourself to do this.

At this point it would be useful to look at the components above
to see where your weaknesses may lie. Ask yourself these questions:

- **In which area or areas are you weakest?**
- **Are you too impulsive and do you tend to move too quickly
  from your gut instinct to action?**
- **Do you disregard or distrust your gut instinct?**
- **Do you let relevant past experiences help you, or do irrelevant
  ones barge in and throw you off track?**
- **Have you learned which types of comebacks work best for you
  and which don't, in order to save some time in formulating
  one?**
- **Do you think of short- and long-term goals and consider the
  big picture as needed?**

There are more questions you might ask yourself, but this set will
help you assess your inclinations, strengths, and weaknesses. It's a
good start toward becoming a communication detective and exercis-
ing your gut instinct in the process of making a comeback decision.
Here are a few examples of some people who have learned to use
their gut instinct in the workplace.

Gut Instinct on Moral Issues

Kathryn Martin, career consultant and board of trustees chair for a technical training institute, knows the importance of allowing your gut sense to help you when deciding what to do and say at work. A few years ago she was working to facilitate the hiring of a new CEO, the most important step in an organization's strategy for moving forward. In the midst of this important endeavor, however, she began to get phone calls from senior female faculty alleging that one of the more senior male faculty members was engaging in behaviors contrary to the values of the organization. Martin was trying to "steward the organization forward" and here was someone dragging it back. And she knew that the best CEO candidates wouldn't be attracted to an organization with problems like the ones emerging.

"For me my instincts were strong about what needed to occur," Martin said, "I just needed my head to catch up with them. As a board member I had to sensitively manage the information I was receiving, make sure it was accurate, but also move quickly to make it stop. To do otherwise would have caused friction on the board, possibly made the organization liable, and certainly would have harmed the new hiring process.

"I sensed the immediacy of the situation," Martin told me, "but at the same time knew not to be rash as every rock I picked up would likely lead to other salamanders rushing out. The sense of when to act is often an instinctual thing—one you employ with counsel from others. I had to act with urgency but manage perceptions. I didn't want to do unnecessary harm to the person or destroy his career, but at the same time if we didn't take clear action, stories would surface and the situation would go from bad to worse."

People got behind her and the entire incident was handled within a short time. I asked Martin how she was able to avoid both overreacting and, on the flip side, getting bogged down in information. "I'm more practical than logical," she told me. "My friends say I'm very relationship oriented. I can see the big picture and focus on that rather than the immediate problem alone." Yet on the other hand, she explained, "I don't do a lot of second-guessing myself, worrying if things aren't perfect."

Martin's ability to be practical while also trusting her gut instincts may come from a way of thinking that so many of us do not achieve. She told me, "I don't think of mistakes as failure but rather as a part of learning. I'm always ready to give myself the grace or forgiveness I give others."

This is how balancing gut instinct with useful information is accomplished. You can't be always worried about saying the wrong thing, because now and then it's going to happen. Martin is confident that she has available a repertoire of comebacks that can help her if she slips up. But she also knows that it's unwise to just rush in where only fools tread. It's not easy to reach this skill level at which you're confident about your ability to handle difficult situations as well as any slipups you might make along the way. But it's well worth the effort, and it's an important part of becoming proficient at comebacks.

Gut Instinct Drawn from Prior Experience

A former advisor to presidents and high-powered Washington attorney explained to me how he looks at difficult decisions, including how to choose a comeback: "Successful people look at things as jigsaw puzzles and keep rearranging the pieces." Each event may seem a separate, new puzzle, but a lot of what's learned from previous ones can be used again and again. When people forget this, when they treat each circumstance as completely unique, they can't use their gut because they lack the benefit of historical knowledge.

You have to build on the past, try what worked before in a situation similar to the present one. See where it takes you. Take it in steps if you like, going with your gut, but doing so gingerly. Or even try telling the other person, *"I was in a situation not so different from this one a few years back, and this is what we did."*

Effective comebacks, then, usually are a combination of logical and emotional assessments. This can be done quite quickly by those who've trained themselves, seemingly without thinking, to do a logical and emotional check of what comes to their minds when they are affronted or challenged in some way.

Gut Instincts in Inflexible Situations

Michael Freiberg, advertising director for a major computer products company, uses his gut to sense when he's in an inflexible situation.

If you sense that the other party has no room to move (and you know going to your boss or up the line won't work), then give in graciously. You have to learn when to fold. Say something like "I know this isn't what I really need for my department, but I understand that it's what the company needs to do." You don't want to be like a bad child. You have to know when to stop fighting for something. I am always able to walk away feeling okay if I can say to myself: "I may not agree with that decision, but I understand why it was made." I find it very useful to detach myself from those decisions. They are business ones and I let them go. You have to start fresh every day. This lets you keep open and honest communication with people.

Freiberg taps into his emotions to sense when he should cease to push against something with which he disagrees, but he also creates a kind of "emotional clean slate" each day in order not to carry baggage that will cause him to lash out later about something that he could have brought to closure earlier on. Some people can respond with silence or appear to acquiesce but still carry the negative feelings for long periods. Then, one day, when they least expect it, these feelings cause them to come back at someone in a way that is over the top. So emotions, when used to sense what's called for in a situation, are helpful, but residual resentments for having to acknowledge and respond to them in a less than desired way are not.

Gut Instinct Relying on Learned Clues

Bill Evans—lawyer, former brewing company executive, and entrepreneur—attributes the knowledge of when to push and when to back off to age and experience. "When you're younger you want to move faster and not tolerate fools lightly. I learned when appointed to my first board of directors that there is usually a long view and more to the issues than you initially think. I began to have more patience and made fewer rapid-fire decisions."

Evans senses a "line in the sand," which he describes as an instinct or a feel for when an issue is too small to make a big deal out of it or to warrant a strong reaction. One rule that helps him detect this line is to ask himself: "If I don't confront, will I feel badly about myself?"

It's tough enough at work to try to make sure emotions are neither over the top nor ignored when responding to difficult situations. But what about when it's a matter of life and death? That's what it amounts to sometimes when we're patients dealing with doctors. And looking at this dire type of situation can be helpful at work, too, when we feel something is a life-or-death issue in terms of our careers.

Dr. Jerome Groopman, in his book *How Doctors Think*, describes how our success level when communicating with doctors depends on our ability to gauge their emotional temperaments. Groopman wrote:

> *Typically, it is the doctor who assesses the patient's emotional state. But few of us realize how strongly a physician's mood and temperament influence his medical judgment. We, of course, may get only glimpses of our doctor's feelings, but even those brief moments can reveal a great deal about why he chose to pursue a possible diagnosis or offered a particular treatment.*[8]

Patients usually have a short period of time to obtain a diagnosis during a visit. Medicine, after all, is a business, and time is money. Doctors start the process the moment they lay eyes on you. Groopman warns that doctors rely on shortcut thinking that allows them to quickly cut through irrelevant information. Such techniques are known as "heuristics." Within minutes of first seeing a patient, doctors can have in mind two or three possible diagnoses. That means, as it does in a job interview, that the first few minutes are crucial. And before those even occur, patients need to know how the doctor is likely to see them. Will he notice first that you have good color, are attractive, energetic, personable, and not terribly sick-looking at all? And if he or she does, will you provide enough information early on to counter that erroneous impression? After all, you are there to see him because you're ill. But he may have seen a lot of very ill people before you and so you're looking good to him. Patients need to know if this happens to them regularly and causes their illness to be overlooked.

Here we're talking about a very high-level skill. As if it isn't enough to engage in the employment of gut instincts and the other components in the model on page 129, the truly effective communicator is able to empathize—to get into the mind of the other person and so sense how his or her gut instinct (with regard to comeback decision-making) is operating. If people formulate quick impressions of you that are incorrect, then you need to make sure additional, key information is provided before the wrong conclusion is drawn. In short, it's valuable to know how to sense what another person is sensing about you. If you're young, for example, and you can tell someone is underestimating you because of your youth, then you'll want to say and do things that make him pause and reflect on his surface impression. Why get angry? People often underestimate the young, so it's nothing personal. But you need to know if that's happening.

If other people are capable of reacting to you on the basis of small amounts of information, then it's likely true of you as well. It's important to know yourself—your emotional self—and how quick you are to rely on it or disregard it. Anyone wanting to become more proficient at comebacks should do a self-assessment of his or her emotions. Here are some questions to ask yourself as a way of determining whether you are as yet in a good place for understanding your emotions and gut instinct. Only then can you assemble a personal comeback repertoire and apply it effectively.

COMEBACK EMOTIONAL READINESS QUESTIONS

Generally speaking:

1. Do I fully appreciate my emotional self?
2. Do I fail to learn from emotional input that has worked and not worked for me?
3. Have I developed emotional flexibility—a range of responses?
4. Am I in need of a fair amount of catch-up practice in sensing anticipatory clues?
5. Do I pride myself too much on being a logical person?

6. Have I fostered an appreciation of my gut instincts?
7. Do I insist that people act logically, as if that is somehow better?
8. Am I attentive to how other people's gut instincts influence what they say and do, and do I take that into consideration when responding?
9. Have I devoted sufficient time to developing my awareness of the emotional contexts in which I function at work?
10. Would people who know me say I should develop more awareness about the emotional input and impact of what I say and do at work?

Place your answers here:

(1)_____ (2)_____ (3)_____ (4) _____ (5) _____
(6) _____ (7) _____ (8) _____ (9) _____ (10)_____

Yes answers to 1, 3, 6, 8, and 9 above are good, as are *no* answers to the remainder. Of course, this is just a rough guide. But you can use it to focus your efforts on improving your comeback emotional readiness or, to put it another way, your communication gut instinct development.

Even if you aced this little inventory, there's much more to learn, but you're off to a strong start with regard to letting your gut instincts be part of your mastery of comebacks. Now we'll look at how to employ your logic and gut instincts in finding and using comebacks that help you engage in conflict and come away completely—or at least largely—unscathed.

CHAPTER EIGHT

When Conflict Is Inevitable

Conflict is inevitable at some time for everyone at work. People disagree. There are ways, however, some we've already discussed, of doing so without making matters worse. There are ways to disagree constructively and to prevent other people from causing us to respond in disagreeable ways.

TAKING YOURSELF OUT OF DISAGREEMENTS

As important as it is to allow your gut to have a say in your choice of comebacks, it's also important not to allow that emotional component of your personality to lead you toward creating situations that are needlessly "personal." References to yourself and your feelings should be avoided unless they facilitate your goals—namely, those times when discussing emotions is required to help "clear the air" of grudges or bad feelings in difficult situations.

We discussed earlier not allowing yourself to become defensive. But there are more aspects to separating yourself from the problem, and this chapter examines a host of them.

Getting Rid of the "I" and "Me"

There is one easy clue to recognizing this bad habit. If you hear yourself using the words "I" or "me" more than occasionally during a heated discussion, you probably own the problem without even intending to do so. Below is a conversation that shows how easy it is to fall into the trap of owning a problem that could be shared were it not for one party's reliance (in this case Marion's) on personal pronouns. In my classes and workshop sessions, I've referred to this as "taking the whole monkey on your back."

> Marion: What you just said is very upsetting to me.
> Bill: In what way?
> Marion: I wasn't doing anything and you came along and insulted me.
> Bill: Aren't you being oversensitive?
> Marion: I'm not oversensitive.
> Bill: Seems that way.
> Marion: If you were me, you'd think differently.

Clearly Marion is taking quite personally something that Bill has said. The problem is less that she is doing so than that her expression of those feelings refers back so repeatedly to herself. In so doing, she completely fails to place the burden of apology or explanation on Bill. Instead, she talks only about herself and her own point of view. Hearing herself use "I" and "me" more than one or two times should be a signal to her that she has personalized a problem instead of letting Bill know that *he* said something he shouldn't have. Since she fails to notice, Bill is able to keep the focus on her rather than on the problem.

Too often, people allow their feelings, or their reactions, to become the focus of a discussion rather than the real issue. It's more likely to occur with women, but men are not immune. It usually allows the person who's caused the offense to wriggle out of having to explain, apologize, and change his or her ways.

"Why don't you like my approach?" may seem like an innocuous question, but it invites rejection of *your* proposed action. Rewording the question to something like *"What would you change in that approach?"* removes any personal reference. The focus then becomes the issue at hand, rather than who's introduced it.

In contrast to the conversation above, imagine if it had happened this way:

Marion: Bill, you went too far this time.
Bill: Did I upset you?
Marion: What you said was way over the line, by any standard.
Bill: You're awfully sensitive.
Marion: Don't let it happen again, Bill.

In this group of responses, Marion has not once mentioned her emotions, and there are no references to *"I"* or *"me."* She has placed the focus squarely on Bill's actions and on what he needs to do to correct them.

The next time you hear yourself using "I" or "me," pause to think. As a rule, don't talk about being upset, frustrated, or annoyed, nor should you in some other way imply that you're feeling emotional about the issue at hand. Instead, go after the issue: "This has happened before and it can't happen again"; "This is a mistake that needs to be fixed"; and "Let's look at what happened here and make sure it doesn't happen again"—these are a few effective ways of keeping the focus *off* your emotions and *on* the problem.

Here are some more:

"Let's focus on the issue, not on your perceptions of me."

"I'll be happy to talk about our feelings after we've solved the problem."

"This can only be solved by focusing on the solution and ignoring the distractions."

"But," you might ask, "what if the issue *is* my emotions or those of the other person?" That's a fair question. But even then, it is possible to present problems as being partly yours but also of import to the organization in which you work. Here are some ways to take someone's attempt to accuse you of a weakness—being too serious—and turn it around to your benefit:

"You bet I'm taking this seriously. Aren't you?"

"If you mean this issue has my attention, you're absolutely right,"

"And your point is . . . ?"

Here is an example of how the third line above might be used. Someone with whom you work is angry. He says, *"You always have to have the last word,"* to you. Now, maybe this is more true than not. If so, you might want to alter that behavior, because it renders you too predictable—and likely annoying. But perhaps he is simply angry and shooting from the hip. You could reply, smiling, *"And your point is . . . ?"* You get his point, but use humor to give him a chance to rethink his comment. If he doesn't want to insult you, he'll take the opportunity and perhaps laugh.

If you're feeling particularly generous or want very much to get back to the major issues at hand, instead of what's been said about your penchant for wanting to have the last word, it's possible to say, "We've been nearly of one mind to this point, so it seems a shame to wander off that track when we're so close to a solution."

The take-away here is that you don't have to address the insult and thereby make it personal. Having the last word can be seen as something good, too. So by responding in this way, you're essentially saying that you're not taking his observation as an insult (even though you may know that is exactly how it was intended).

What if he doesn't think you're funny? He might say, "*You know what I mean. You don't know when to shut up.*" Okay, now we're on different ground. Even so, you could still avoid altercation with: "*My wife says that, too.*" Also, although it may come across as missing the point, you might try instead: "*Perhaps I do tend to talk a bit more when I'm passionate about something.*" This agrees with the premise of the critic's comment but is an introspective response rather than a defensive or aggressive one.

Let's say he won't let it drop. He then says, "*A bit? You can't control yourself.*"

Now we're getting to the point where he probably deserves all you've got. But wait, you're practicing here. What else could you say that might bring you both back to the issue at hand? How about one of the following:"*Oh, I'm in control of myself, believe me.*" This lets him know that you are trying to avoid anger. He may be so immersed in his own view of things that he hasn't noticed that you are beginning to find this line of discussion less than appealing and that you could escalate it to an argument if that is what he wants. After a brief silence, you could follow this with: "*I'll take your advice, think it over, and see what I can do about that last-word part, but for now let's go back to the project.*" Another alternative, because you're practicing:"*That happens. But, believe me, you're not perfect either. And yet somehow we go on. So let's do that now. What do you think we should do about x?*"

Using this approach, you don't deny that there is some validity in what he has said, but you calmly remind him that the problem is not yours alone, and then endeavor to move the interaction back to the issue you two were attempting to solve before he accused you of always needing to have the last word. Another option is this: *I guess this is where we ask ourselves whether our task is to fix me or to fix the problem we came here to discuss. I vote for the latter.*

This comeback diverts attention away from the emotional aspect of the discussion and back to the objective one. That takes some intestinal fortitude. Part of you wants to slap him down, but instead you rise above that inclination and remind him (and yourself—by using "we" instead of "I") that there is a larger work-related issue on which you both should focus. You might also try one other option:

> "I'm going to take your advice and think about that "having-the-last-word" habit. It's probably something I can change, and you might even help me do it."

This is a conversion of insult to advice in which you've accepted his premise to a degree and enlisted him in the solution. You're now a team. Now you can go back to the project you're working on. You see, you've limited his choices here, if he isn't completely unaware of rules in conversation. If you cause yourself to lose face a bit, as you do here by agreeing to work on the last-word habit, according to the unstated rules of reciprocity in human interaction, he is not supposed to force your "face" down further but rather pick you up a bit. He might say nothing and move on to the work at hand; or he might kindly agree to help you control the habit you've so graciously offered to fix.

Thinking Along with Your Opposition

While it isn't good, as a rule, to describe your own emotional state while addressing a problem, it can be a mistake to not attend to and deal with the emotional state or emotional point of view of those people who differ with you. As mentioned earlier, there are times when emotions need to be addressed.

Michael J. Fox was at the peak of a hugely successful acting career when he developed Parkinson's disease at an early age. It thrust him into a new way of life—that of helping to find a cure for Parkinson's via his work with the Michael J. Fox Foundation. As anyone who follows the news understands, one of the greatest current challenges to finding a cure for Parkinson's disease has been the controversy over whether it is morally correct to use human embryos to extract stem cells for research and potential medical use. Fox was convinced that embryos, especially those that would be discarded anyway, should be used to help cure an array of diseases, including Parkinson's.

In his book *Always Looking Up*, Michael J. Fox displayed the important skill of letting the other side of the argument be at least partially right and to reasonably portray its point of view. Rather than attack and disparage those who oppose his position, he endeavored to regard them as having a right to do so. Fox even went so far as to find ways in which he and they were in agreement:

> *I have a stake in this argument that some may fairly say disqualifies me from giving both sides of the argument equal weight. You yourself may have thoughtfully considered the issue and arrived at the conclusion that embryonic stem cell research is wrong and that, at the very least, it is not something you want the government to support. As frustrated as we in the patient community are . . . so too are you frustrated that we, the proponents, just don't get it,*

that we're missing the bigger picture. In that way, we two can em-
pathize with each other, while not agreeing. This is why I brought
into the political arena my concerns and my hopes that this work
can produce cures and treatments, not to shame or ridicule those
who disagree with me, and not to use the bully pulpit of celebrity
to drown out anyone else's voice. The opposite is true. . . . And as
much as I want to make my own points, to express my own needs
and desires, I know it's critical that differing opinions be given
equal hearing.[1]

With important exceptions, in most workplaces the issues involved rarely rise to the level of life and death, as the subject of
embryonic stem cell research has for people on both sides of that
question. Yet often enough at work—and I mean all kinds of work,
not only for-profit—we become deeply invested in our own views.
So it *can* feel something like a life-or-death issue when our career or
our leadership will be threatened if we don't win a certain argument.

Fox's expressed view, hard as it may be at times for him to maintain, is that people who believe life begins at conception (and so
oppose embryonic stem cell research) nevertheless have something
in common with himself. He might have seen only differences, and
could have perceived them as blocking his quest for a cure for Parkinson's disease. But he didn't.

This kind of frame of mind allows for debate and discussion.
While it doesn't give ground in terms of where each stands on the
issue, it builds a bridge based on empathy for each side's commitment and passion.

Just as separating yourself from the problem is important, inte-
grating the other person's view with yours as a way of solving it is a
useful way of making progress with people who are blocking you.

Supreme Court Justice Ruth Bader Ginsburg once said of making progress on the Supreme Court, "You have to persuade four

of your colleagues to get your voice heard." Imagine that. Even someone like Justice Ginsburg has to make sure she connects what matters to her to what matters to four other justices before she can make progress toward influencing their decisions. She added that otherwise she gets a "Dear Ruth" letter, essentially a rejection of her views.[2] So what can the rest of us take from this? Link your ideas to those of others you wish to persuade and you're more likely to succeed. And this applies to comebacks as well.

My son came up to me shortly before I was about to write this section and said, "You got the wrong cold medicine yesterday." He's usually more adept at communicating than that but he wasn't feeling well. I knew what he meant. He meant that the medicine his sister and I purchased the day before for him was not the one he'd been using successfully the prior few days. But by putting the word "you" at the front of his observation, he made it a complaint. And if as his mother I wasn't used to interpreting what he meant to say, I would have been hard-pressed not to say, "You're eighteen. Buy your own medicine next time," or something to that effect. Why? Because of the way he conveyed his message. Put "you" in front of a complaint and you're more often than not asking for a defensive response. Use "we" or "It looks like" instead, and progress is more likely.

This is very important. Making other people feel that they're wrong, and especially that you're right by virtue of their error, is rarely effective. Take this simple example provided by my son. Had he said, "Mom, we got the wrong medicine yesterday," or "The medicine bought yesterday isn't working as well as the one I had before," he would have avoided possible offense. In truth, "we" did not buy the medicine. I did. But "we" would imply that he may have played a role in this error by perhaps not having made his request sufficiently specific.

I mention this episode from my personal life here because I've found that it pertains to what frequently happens in the workplace.

Every office has someone who, when a task isn't completed to his liking, resorts to inflammatory statements like *"You didn't do that right"* rather than more helpful statements such as *"Something isn't quite right here"* or *"Let's look at this again from a different angle."* These people fail to recognize that chances are good that when someone is wrong about something, they're only partially so.

In much the same way as I viewed my son's complaint about my purchasing the incorrect medicine, I also find that managers often complain about people who don't listen to their instructions—only to realize, through coaching, that they themselves really weren't communicating clearly. Returning to Carol Smith, senior VP of Elle, when asked what she is learning to do less often, she replied:

> *Less of the "I want to know who did that. Who decided to give that rate to that person?" I want less of that self-righteousness. I have a little bit of that, and I think I'd like to have less of that— the "You see? I told you so." That's definitely something I should work on.*[3]

Presenting information so that people can digest it and then getting their reaction is a way to begin doing less "telling it like it is," which often makes people defensive. Instead, listening for a hook in what they say in response to the point or points you're trying to make—a way to use what they're saying to convey your own perspective—is usually much more effective.

Constructing a bridge in the midst of discord is a wonderful comeback tool. If you really listen, you'll find that in most of what people say to each other there are points where agreement can be found. The problem is that most people fail to notice them.

It takes practice to locate points of agreement in the midst of dissension. And there's no time like the present to do exactly that. After all, this strategic technique can enable comebacks that keep relationships intact, help to save face for both parties involved, and move discussion forward.

Getting Past Derision

My husband likes to remind me of the time in Lisbon, Portugal, when he sat in the back row of a huge auditorium where I was about to step onstage. It was an international business leaders' conference attended by hotshots from around the world. Glass-faced translator booths lined the auditorium on both sides. A massive screen at the rear of the stage projected the image of the speaker to the back rows.

And then up the steps to the stage climbed five-foot-five-inch me—blond, slight, and appearing in their eyes as someone from whom they were unlikely to learn much. At least that's how many of these business leaders responded when I took the stage because many present were used to male experts. My husband watched as, one after another, many of them closed their notebooks and put down their pencils. I noticed some of it as well, and I knew what they were thinking. This was not the first audience of mostly men from other countries who'd responded to me this way.

But I knew, too, that if things went as planned I was about to make their day. If I could get past the first few moments of doubt and give them some of my best stuff, delivered powerfully, then I knew the audience would be in my hands. And, indeed, that is just what happened. One by one, those same men who'd closed their notebooks reopened them. They laughed when I joked, their eyes were glued to the stage, and the presentation was a success. Once I finished speaking, I could hardly get out of the auditorium so the next speaker could come onstage, for all the people surrounding me with praise, questions, and invitations to their countries.

Sometimes you just have to get on with it. Bypass the negative first impressions of you or your ideas. See and hear yourself as they might because they don't know you or what you can deliver. Then you aren't surprised at their initial reaction and are less inclined to take it personally and have it negatively affect your performance.

Not many of us will ever forget Susan Boyle, a heavyset, middle-aged woman from a small village in Scotland, who strode with confidence onto the stage of *Britain's Got Talent* in 2009.[4] The people in the audience were already laughing before Boyle ever opened her mouth. When she answered the judges' questions in a "cheeky" way, they laughed even more loudly and some rolled their eyes. But when Boyle began to sing, the crowd went absolutely quiet. Tears began to fill the eyes of audience members and judges alike, as the underestimated songstress dazzled them with her astounding talent. The YouTube posting of Boyle's performance received millions of hits. She became an overnight show business sensation.

What would have happened if Boyle had responded to the initial laughs, jeers, and dismissive facial reactions that audience members and judges made at her appearance? What if those unkind responses had shaken her confidence because, actually, they were quite personal in nature? Asked afterward how she could sing in the face of so many people making fun of her, she replied, "I just got on with it." And she did.

It's not easy for most of us to be like Susan Boyle—to let derision roll off our shoulders and just plow onward. But anyone who wants to be successful at comebacks needs to know how sensitive he or she is to such things. If you're down at the bottom of the toughness scale in this regard, you are going to miss many of your goals because you won't be able to get past others doubting, criticizing, and even mocking you. If, however, you expect and prepare for the possibility of such treatment, if you can move forward, confident that the scoffers and naysayers will soon be changing their tune, you'll have a much better chance of getting what you want.

To Put It in Your Words

You have to ask yourself sometimes, as mentioned before, if an offensive comment ought simply to be made part of a positive response as an alternative to waging war over it.

Being able to do this effectively is a truly valuable skill. Here's an example of how Tom Vestry, hospital administrator, employed it:

> *I had an annual performance evaluation by our hospital CEO. The evaluation was going well but they usually save up one "gotcha" item that they can discuss with you. The CEO said, "I understand from your staff that you show favoritism to one of your staff members." I thought for a second and said, "Yes, I do show favoritism. I favor staff that are dedicated, productive, team players, and loyal. This staff member has volunteered to work on difficult projects and did what was necessary to complete the projects even if it required long periods of working sixty to eighty hours a week."*
>
> *The CEO must have agreed with me as he used this same argument ("favoring" the hardworking) when the subject came up in a future management team meeting (not concerning my employee).*

This example emphasizes again that tweaking the meaning of a critic's words to make your own point can be particularly effective. I've taught this in my negotiation classes. Rather than fight everything someone says, even if the comment is intended as an insult, consider using at least part of it in your reply. Had Vestry defended himself, said something like, *"I never show favoritism"* or *"Who told you that? It isn't true,"* he would not have succeeded as he did in convincing the CEO that what he'd been doing was giving attention to a promising employee rather than playing favorites. Those are two very different things.

Consider, for example, if someone were to say, *"You're stubborn."* You could reply defensively:

"No I'm not."

"I'm not the only one."

"What! I'm always keeping an open mind."

But the word "stubborn" is merely a word. It describes a set of behaviors that from a slightly different vantage point might be described as persistent, determined, focused, involved, concerned, or tenacious. As we've discussed, words can be weak vehicles of meaning. People use them incorrectly for many reasons. So why fight an incorrect word or phrase when you can replace it with your own word(s) or a different meaning? For example, in response to the stubborn remark, it's possible to reply:

"I am persistent, that's for sure."

"You got me there, I'm tenacious when an issue's as important as this."

"I'd say all of us here are stubborn because we want the best possible outcome."

This takes practice. You need to listen carefully to what people say to pull from it a positive link to the position you want to convey. Some people want to trip you up by labeling what you're saying or doing in negative ways. If you fall for it, you derail the progress you might otherwise make in a negotiation or a relationship.

WHEN WORDS ALONE WON'T DO

Facial expressions and gestures can stand alone as comebacks and often are much more effective than words. Unlike most words, it's difficult to take them literally, because they are often fleeting. Besides, while people can repeat the words of others, most have trouble mimicking a facial expression or gesture in exactly the same way it was conveyed, so it can be used to hint. Erving Goffman referred to both words and nonverbal expressions used ambiguously as forms of "tact." The meaning of what is said or not said but rather expressed is in the deniable range of communication, but it can nevertheless have a very significant impact.[5]

"I'm just not the direct type," an international business attorney told me. But if you assume that means he can't go for the jugular, you'd be wrong. He is truly impressive and in high demand. When other people might rant and rave, he told me, he's more likely to quietly look at whoever has offended him or proposed too low an offer during negotiation, not in their eyes, but somewhere that makes them change their tune—at the bridge of their nose.

This is how he says it works. "If you're ever eyeballing someone down, never look into his eyes. Look at the top of the nose. Don't wince. They get the impression that you're staring at them and they turn their eyes down more quickly. You have to practice it. And it becomes a really handy point especially in a group. You eyeball somebody across the table, looking at the bridge of the nose. After a while you can do it easily." He added, "It's funny that if someone is more vociferous or forceful, they think they're making progress, but I make more progress staring at their nose. It weakens even these people. They won't raise their eyes. It's a way of downing a guy without shouting at him."

I asked him if part of the power of this technique is that it is deniable later. He agreed and said, "And no one will admit that this technique had an effect on them." It works for this attorney because he would rather not shout someone down, but clearly he is not averse to intimidating someone nonverbally.

There are many other nonverbal comebacks that are every bit as powerful as verbal ones, if not more so. You can produce and practice some of these by simply thinking about someone saying something that is offensive. Stand before a mirror and watch your facial expressions as you think of times like these. You may see yourself raising your left eyebrow, slightly narrowing the right eye, tilting the head to the right, mouth slightly bowed upward. When you're particularly taken aback these moves conjoined with a sudden pull backward as if surprised produces a look that says something along the lines of: *"What was that about?"* or *"You're kidding me, right?"* The beauty of such expressions is that should someone respond with, "What was that look all about," you have the option to say, *"I was confused for a moment there," "I was thinking about what you just said," "I was a bit surprised,"* or *"I'm still sorting that out myself."*

We have a host of these time-buying and warning expressions. Just looking surprised can often be enough to cause the other person to rephrase what he or she just said. You can always rest your elbow on a desk or table, your index finger at temple and thumb at chin, your head tilted and looking down, as if trying to figure out what just happened. This can be followed by cupping your chin, index finger above it and thumb below, looking either off into the distance or right at the person with a perplexed expression, and then waiting for him to come through with a rephrasing or explanation. Again you've bought yourself time or warned him that he needs to rethink and adjust what he just said.

Crossing your arms on a desk and leaning forward somewhat when someone has said something a tad insulting will send a signal that you're on the offense. Accompanied by a direct look, a solemn expression, and waiting for what's coming next can signal the need to halt or change conversational tone or direction. Some people allow their fingers to click on the desk, pinky first, the next three fingers following, a few times to signal increased aggravation or agitation. We all do these things now and then, and it's important to learn which nonverbal expressions work for you. Think about which ones make people stop and reconsider what they've said, or which ones make them ask you why you appear to be angry or upset.

These are just a few nonverbal expressions that can make a big difference in how you're received. If you're good with words but your facial expressions and/or gestures don't send effective complementary signals, you're not yet a master of comebacks. You may be verbally adept, but your body defeats you. Truly gifted people are aware of both verbal and nonverbal expressions and make sure that the two work together, or, if one is working alone, that the other does not negate the intended message.

In addition to using the right expressions to package your comebacks, you can also benefit from gaining the ability to suppress reactive expressions or gestures, the ones that give away initial feelings. For example, most people's voices get higher when they're nervous. We also tend to swallow more, and that can be perceived as a sign that we're about to cave under pressure. We may squint with anger before having a chance to think about it, so here again practice is important. A poker face is a valuable thing for more than just playing cards. If you can train your bodily reactions to pause, just long enough for your now comeback-educated brain to decide how to proceed, you'll be ahead of most people. And you won't be able to be read like an open book.

Breathing in is one way to stop from reacting in a dysfunctional nonverbal way. Essentially you're busying your body so it can't do what it does automatically. Looking off to the side for a moment as if thinking is another. Scratching your head can buy a moment, as can reaching to fix a cuff or tie a shoe. Some people prefer to stand up and walk, and some even cup the back of their necks as they walk, again as if thinking about what has been said. After a while, you'll be able to pause and reflect without these crutches, but they help at first. And they're useful when the thing said by the other person is so out of line that anyone would need help being silent in word and action. I sometimes smile a bit—just a bit—when someone has said something that's a bit rude. The smile shouldn't be sarcastic. Rather it should appear that you've noted an insult and you're considering your response.

Later we'll look again at nonverbal aspects of comebacks. People don't just *say* things. They express things by words and actions. So it's important to understand how you express yourself nonverbally. You can deny thinking a certain way, but if people see it written all over your face, they're not going to believe you. Better to know how you look and gesture, because people are going to take those into account when reacting and responding to you. People astute at comebacks use their expressions to their advantage rather than remaining in the dark about at least half of their communication.

MAKING PEOPLE FEEL BIGGER

We thought we'd end this chapter by going a step beyond agreeing with an adversary to actually making him or her feel good. Usually that's the last thing on our minds when we're disagreeing with people. But as has already been argued here, it shouldn't be.

When Senator Ted Kennedy passed away, there were many tributes to him, among them one from his longtime friend Vice President Joseph Biden. When asked why conservatives who were politically opposed to Ted Kennedy liked him, Biden replied, "He was never petty, never small. He always made you feel bigger."[6]

Senator John McCain added to this. He and Kennedy had had

some spirited debates, but they embraced at the end of each, went on to the next battle, and found ways to work together for the good of the country. This kind of focus renders pettiness a nonstarter. And Kennedy, despite his passion, was a master at assuring that the "face" of most who opposed him was not the target. According to McCain, Ted Kennedy put the interests of his country first, which meant what others would take or make personal, Kennedy endeavored to treat as part of the process of debate.[7]

Ronald Reagan was the "great communicator" president for similar reasons. He would express anger publicly at times but would use humor freely. During a 1980 presidential debate with Reagan, then president Jimmy Carter raised the issue of Reagan's controversial position on the Medicare bill. Reagan didn't get angry or allow himself to be drawn into a negative discussion. Instead he smiled and said, "There you go again." It struck many people as quite humorous, especially for a presidential debate. It was flippant, but only slightly so. When President Reagan was asked in 1989 by journalist Jim Lehrer if he'd practiced or in some way planned to say that memorable line, the president replied that it just seemed the thing to say at the time to something so repetitious.[8]

He was quick with humor and optimistic, which "often neutralized his ideological foes." After Reagan was shot by John W. Hinckley, Jr., two months into his presidency, he joked with the doctors about to operate on him, saying, "I hope you're all Republicans." And later he told his worried wife, Nancy, "Honey, I forgot to duck." In the 1984 election, his age had become an issue. In a televised presidential debate, the seventy-three-year-old Reagan turned to Senator Walter Mondale, his opponent, and said: "I'm not going to exploit for political purposes my opponent's youth and inexperience." It got a laugh from likely everyone present, including Mondale.[9]

This skill is related to the one we started with in this chapter. Refocusing a problem so that you don't present yourself as personally responsible or emotionally involved is important. If all parties or groups address a problem as being something outside themselves, even though they are involved or even responsible, progress is usually made more quickly and more effectively. That's why it's important to avoid comebacks that make things personal unless you have to "burn" someone, or let yourself be burned once, in order to move on. But those situations should be rare. If they aren't, you might be working in a politically pathological place. If that works for you and your stress level, go for it. Otherwise, you might want to move on.

In the next two chapters we will step away from emphasis on comebacks that suit the person using them and look at how you can select ones that work well with the person or people with whom you're conversing and that suit the situation. You'll meet Rachel Rongwhey, a fictional character, but one based on so many people I've met. Rachel hasn't a clue about how to do these things and so her career is headed for derailment. She can save herself, but it won't be easy.

CHAPTER NINE

Pulsing the Other Person

Rachel Rongwhey's mind was racing as she drove to work the Tuesday morning that marked her third month as Wastenot Industries' manager of large bin sales. The day before, she'd received a memo from her boss accusing her of delaying the latest bin launch with her "endless list of questions" that she'd "saved for the day before the launch." Her boss, Marilyn, had never sent a memo like this before and hadn't said anything in the past about her eve-of-launch questions, which Rachel had posed for the purpose of being thorough.

Rachel believes in addressing issues up front rather than dealing with crises later on. She'd learned from another job that a critical memo can be a sign of bad things to come. She would not make the same mistake of thinking the recent memo was not serious.

Rachel had read the memo over and over again during the night, fuming about Marilyn's choice of words. How dare she single her out when others had questions, too. Sure, hers were the most extensive—yes, "extensive," but hardly "endless." And she certainly didn't want to hold things up. She glared at the word "saved." Marilyn wouldn't have chosen that word had she not intended to insult me, Rachel thought. At Wastenot, the cardinal sin was to waste anything, including time. "Here at Wastenot," their CEO had told them only last week, "we waste nothing, and that is why we are so successful. It is also why I will only speak for a few minutes, so we can all get back to doing our jobs well."

Rachel had decided the night before that she would not ignore this attack and would confront her boss today. After all, Marilyn herself was to blame for the long time it took to launch the master bin. Rachel would not, she promised herself, take that monkey on her back.

The use of e-mail really bothered Rachel, too. And it was sent just before Marilyn left for home. Rachel muttered about how Marilyn knew sending it at that late hour would prevent resolving the problem until the next day. She knew Rachel would have to deal with the insult late into the evening. In Rachel's eyes it was a breech of civility. The meeting had been earlier in the afternoon, so Marilyn had had time to walk over to Rachel's office to discuss her concerns. The memo was an insult to Rachel, and what's more, it seemed to be the beginning of a paper trail.

When Rachel arrived at work, she walked past all the people she normally greeted each morning, whispering to herself in anger. She had no time for niceties if this was how she would be treated at what she described in her whispering as a "godforsaken excuse for a business." She'd handled difficult situations before, so people knew that when something serious was on her mind, she would not have time to be a team player. She handled things as soon as they happened and did not waste a moment clearing her name or settling a score. She responded in this way no matter the issue or who had raised it. And she would do the same now. This would not be her problem for long, Rachel thought. Within an hour, Marilyn would be wishing she'd never sent that memo.

Rachel tossed her coat on the rack in her office and headed right off to see Marilyn. Usually she would sit at her desk and recover from rush hour with a decaf coffee. Today was different. She would nip this problem in the bud.

Marilyn was on the telephone, but saw Rachel, smiled, and held up her index finger indicating that she'd be off the phone shortly. Rachel remained at the door, walked back and forth a couple of times, urging Marilyn with her intense expression to finish her call. Marilyn looked puzzled but continued her telephone call. She shrugged her shoulders and held up one of her hands as if to say this could go on for a bit. Rachel remained at the door. She knew that Marilyn could easily get called into a meeting and that this situation needed to be resolved immediately.

Marilyn ended the telephone call and motioned for Rachel to enter her office. At this point Rachel was red in the face and her mouth was tight with annoyance. Marilyn offered Rachel a decaf coffee, which Rachel rejected with an impatient wave of her hand. Marilyn paused. She couldn't miss Rachel's mood. And Rachel was glad of that.

The conversation began:

Marilyn: Rachel, you look upset about something. Is it the memo?

Rachel: What right did you have to send that to me?

Marilyn (looking tired): It was the end of a very long day, Rachel. I had to rush to pick up Billy at preschool. He was not feeling well.

Rachel: I had a long day, too, but didn't blame you for what was clearly, and largely, your fault.

Marilyn: What?

Rachel: I had to think about that memo all night.

Marilyn: I'm your boss, Rachel. It's my job to let you know when something you're doing jeopardizes a project.

Rachel: JEOPARDIZES!

Marilyn: Listen, you're upset, and maybe I should have come to see you or written to arrange a meeting. It was an oversight. Why don't you go back to your office and think about it and we'll meet for lunch?

Rachel: Without me, the master bin launch would be taking even longer.

Marilyn: Rachel, you should take a few minutes in your office.

Rachel: You should have taken a few minutes last night before sending me that accusatory e-mail.

Marilyn: "Accusatory e-mail"? That was an informative e-mail.

Rachel: I'll go back to my office. But we need to deal with this at lunch so it doesn't happen again.

Marilyn (angry now): We'll deal with it.

Rachel left in a huff. She'd made the points she wanted to make. Marilyn had been told. This, Rachel assured herself, would not happen again. Over lunch she would let Marilyn know how she expects to be treated. She wasn't going to fall for some halfhearted excuse for an apology.

The departmental secretary knocked on Rachel's door. She had a folder that Rachel had requested the day before. Rachel motioned for her to enter. As the secretary placed the folder on her desk, Rachel looked directly at her. "This place is a pit," she said. "I don't know how you've worked here for ten years." The secretary said nothing and then left quickly.

Fifteen minutes passed before Rachel opened the folder and began to work. None of the people who worked for her came by. Everyone stayed at their desks for the rest of the morning while Rachel fumed, closing file cabinets forcefully and talking to herself. They'd seen her like this on two other occasions and weren't about to become targets themselves.

A good part of knowing how to respond to a difficult situation is "pulsing" the other person, something the most astute among us do quite quickly. This means sensing the person's mood, style, and receptivity to the kind of information you are about to deliver. Equally important is being sensitive to aspects of a situation that render certain comebacks inappropriate and make others more likely to be effective. This assessing of the situation is crucial in emotional and public situations.

You can tell something may not be quite right if a person's actual physical pulse is running fast. But until you know what he was just doing (perhaps running a marathon) or other pertinent information relevant to his overall health, determining that he needs an ambulance could be premature.

Rachel Rongwhey jumped to conclusions. She made the situation all about her and how she'd been wronged. She didn't stop to consider that this was the first time Marilyn had ever sent her a memo like the one she received. Instead of finding that curious, she took it as accusatory and a form of incivility. Rachel didn't stop to think that perhaps Marilyn had jotted this e-mail in a rush to get somewhere and sent it without giving it adequate thought. Add to that the following:

1. Rachel was relying on her first response; worse, she was employing a negative past experience with a memo of warning to interpret Marilyn's present intensions. It's important to consider past experiences when interpreting an event in the present, but Marilyn is not the person who sent Rachel a hurtful memo at a previous job. Rachel needed to "take the pulse" of her current boss, and she didn't do that.

2. Marilyn looked tired when Rachel was in her office. When Rachel learned that Billy, Marilyn's young son, was ill, she could have checked to see if Marilyn had been worried and

perhaps hadn't slept much of the night, being up with Billy. If so, then the Marilyn who wrote the memo was not the usual Marilyn. Rachel, failing to attune herself to Marilyn's situation, cornered her.

3. Rachel didn't consider her past interactions with Marilyn when it came to placing blame. There wasn't a sufficient track record of inappropriate blame by Marilyn to react with such anger and defensiveness.

4. Marilyn tried to respond with understanding rather than anger when Rachel came to her office. Rachel should have noticed this and not rapidly escalated to argument. Reciprocity in communication dictates that one at least attempt to return kindness and understanding. Rachel violated this rule.

5. Marilyn proposed that Rachel take a break and that they discuss the problem later. Rachel resisted. Her exclusive focus on her own needs got in the way of her taking note of what Marilyn and their relationship needed.

6. All of her statements were one-up ($\Uparrow$). There were no one-down ($\Downarrow$) or one-across ($\Rightarrow$) statements that might have given Marilyn an opportunity to make things better. Why didn't Rachel ask questions or buy time? She decided that she knew Marilyn well enough in three months' time to know she'd intended to do Rachel harm.

Rachel's errors remind me of work by anthropologist Mary Catherine Bateson. She describes the dangers inherent in what she calls "myths of conformity" and "myths of disparity."[1] In the former, we assume that we know people when it is merely an illusion to believe so. Given how long people live, they inevitably change over time. Skilled communicators don't take a "here we go again" attitude as soon as they recognize the beginning of a pattern. They study people and try to make sense of what is going on for this person at this time. They're like astute detectives, skeptical of easy categorizations and alert to the limitations of even their own most assured judgments. They ask questions and put a premium on observation and on updating their perceptions.

That's a tall order. Pulsing doesn't come easily to impulsive people like Rachel, nor to overconfident people. It's the province of the observant and the patient. Especially in American culture, being quiet long enough to get a sense of another person often runs counter to what we're taught. We often like to be the quickest, the best, and to have the last word. And we tend to believe that the person with the best argument wins. By contrast, in my international negotiation classes, Asian students often speak of the importance of process and observation. They often find the quick-to-the-pitch way of their American fellow students unsettling and often unproductive.

When cultures are outcome-oriented, it takes extra effort to see that the right process can give rise to a desirable outcome, even if not necessarily the one we had in mind earlier on. If you are inclined to think in terms of outcomes and only want to get to them as quickly as possible, as Rachel did, you may be doing yourself an injustice by neglecting to pulse the people who will determine whether the desired outcome occurs.

Even if Rachel had entered Marilyn's office with the very same assumptions as in the scenario above, she still could have turned things around by attending to Marilyn's actions. There were a number of choice points (opportunities to favorably redirect a conversation) where Rachel could have turned things around. The first one occurred when she saw that Rachel was talking on the telephone. She could have gone back to her office, especially after seeing that the conversation was taking a while. Pacing back and forth and glowering guaranteed that the conversation would start off in a negative manner. Even if she'd missed that choice point, there were many others during the conversation. Here's how things could have gone.

Marilyn: Rachel, you look upset about something. Is it the memo?

This was the first choice point where Rachel could have made things go better. The fact that Marilyn asked about her being upset, and even asked specifically if it had to do with the memo, suggests that perhaps Marilyn had already reconsidered the memo and wished she hadn't sent it. Here is what Rachel could have said:

Rachel: Yes, I am upset. There is no hiding that. And it's about the memo.

Her response would have been honest. There was no hiding her emotions at this point. But by stopping here, she would have given Marilyn an opportunity to explain why she'd sent the memo or even to say that she wished she hadn't. Instead, Rachel plowed forward with her agenda. And with an angry attack:

Rachel: What right did you have to send that to me?

She misused her choice point by saying this. It was far too strong, given how Marilyn was speaking and acting, especially considering their past relationship. But Rachel still could have turned things around, starting right after Marilyn said:

Marilyn (looking tired): It was the end of a very long day, Rachel. I had to rush to pick up Billy at preschool. He was not feeling well.

This was an important opportunity for Rachel. It takes a rude person or someone obsessed with her own needs to blast past someone's concern about their child. Rachel should have controlled her anger at this point and asked Marilyn about Billy. Even if she couldn't bring herself to be solicitous, she could have asked:

Rachel: Is he okay?

Instead, Rachel's next outburst was an insult to Marilyn and their relationship. She dismissed the concern that Marilyn had shared about Billy—a concern that was perhaps her way of telling Rachel that she'd been preoccupied and had sent a memo to which she would normally have given more thought:

Rachel: I had a long day too but didn't blame you for what was clearly, and largely, your fault.

The rest of the conversation is downhill. There are points where Rachel could have turned things around or at least made them less horrible, but she didn't. If we look at the next few comments, we can see that.

Rachel: I had to think about that memo all night.
Marilyn: I'm your boss, Rachel. It's my job to let you know when something you're doing jeopardizes a project.
Rachel: JEOPARDIZES!

Rachel jumped down Marilyn's throat, so to speak, over the word "jeopardizes." She could have asked:

Rachel: Do you think that strong a word is accurate?

That would have given Marilyn, who has a habit of choosing the wrong words, a chance to rephrase what she meant. Again a choice point was lost and the conversation went from bad to worse, even though Marilyn recommended that Rachel take a break and that they discuss things over lunch. This was a gracious offer from Marilyn, given the circumstances. But Rachel Rongwhey refused to accept it.

This example shows how many opportunities we often have to alter the direction of a conversation. When we fail to recognize our 75 percent responsibility, make assumptions without checking them, and move on through a contentious interaction with only our own needs in mind, things don't go well. By pulsing the other person, we can decide if someone we know is receptive. We can also determine more effectively how to approach them. Rachel did neither of these things, and the likelihood of her previously good relationship with Marilyn continuing was thereby diminished considerably.

PULSING KNOWN AND UNKNOWN PEOPLE

Taking the pulse of an unknown person is, of course, different from taking the pulse of someone you already know. In the former case, there's far more to learn. In the latter, you're often sensing only mood and receptivity, but not character or communication style. In both cases, however, the mind-set of a person who knows how to pulse is one of inquisitiveness rather than defensiveness, asking *What am I dealing with here?*

Basketball great Magic Johnson found himself feeling a bit intimidated when as a young man he first started playing on the same team as the legendary Kareem Abdul-Jabbar. In time, though, he not only got to know Abdul-Jabbar but also started giving him advice. Abdul-Jabbar was known for his irascible temperament, so this would have been risky for most junior teammates.

Johnson remembered as a child having asked Abdul-Jabbar for

his autograph and being brushed off. When Johnson joined the Lakers, Abdul-Jabbar was still doing this to people. Johnson chose the moment carefully and waited until their relationship was well developed and receptivity seemed likely before telling Abdul-Jabbar,

You know, you could be a lot nicer to the fans. It wouldn't cost you anything. Even if you can't sign every autograph, you can acknowledge people, or just say hi. The autograph itself isn't important. It's the contact. Whatever happens during those five seconds is what the other person will remember for the rest of their life.[2]

Abdul-Jabbar didn't suddenly become nice to fans, but he became somewhat nicer. He warmed up a little, according to Johnson. Reading Johnson's memoir, you become aware of his ability to read people, to sense who he is dealing with and adjust his style to them. That's critical to responding in any contentious or potentially contentious situation.

Johnson likely learned some of this from the basketball court. Coach Jack McKinney helped him understand that his biggest mistake was trying to play every guy the same way.[3] Similarly, to be persuasive, you have to be able to take the pulse of the individuals around you, notice their differences, and make that part of your decision-making process when dealing with them.

This is particularly important if you don't know the people well, or at all. Often at work we need to deal with new people. Nonverbal expressions are an important component of pulsing, whether you know the person well or not, but they are especially critical in the latter case, because people often don't say what they mean early in relationships. They engage in a good deal of expected social etiquette, so it's difficult to pulse them without attending closely to body language.

There are many good books on the subject of body language,

but here are a few guidelines that will help before you seek out more extensive information:

1. Attend to the differences between denotative and connotative meanings.
   Think on two levels when assessing what people mean. This was discussed in chapter 6. Review that. And watch for something that just doesn't seem right. Then ask questions to confirm your perceptions, or simply watch the person closely for a while before trusting him.

2. Get a sense of the person's conviction.
   Does the person look directly at you when saying things that could be untrue? Except in cultures where making eye contact is frowned upon, people usually look into each other's eyes when they're comfortable with what they're saying. Look for that. (Though don't discount the possibility that the other person habitually avoids eye contact, or that it may be due to a medical condition.)

3. Pay attention to tone.
   Notice when there is a mismatch between what is being said and the expression or tone that accompanies it. This "disconnect" can signal that the person isn't being forthcoming.

4. Listen for style.
   As with nonverbal communication, there are many good sources on this topic. For example Alan Rowe, Warren Bennis, and I developed a leadership-style inventory and Rowe and I developed a negotiation-style inventory.[4] Below I've included a few examples of different styles from the leadership

style inventory, as demonstrated by a realtor who is trying to sell you a house.

Commanding: *"You have to grab this house now. It won't last long. It's the best on the market in this area."*

Logical: *"Here are some pages of information on the school system, community, prices of other houses in the area, and a host of other things I thought you'd want to know."*

Inspirational: *"I can tell you love this house. Imagine your children scampering through the lovely yard next year."*

Supportive: *"Don't hesitate to ask me anything or to call me at any time. I'll meet you at your place if that's more convenient."*

Simply by attending to how people speak, you can achieve some degree of pulsing, and, at the very least, a successful baseline. While few people use only one style, listening for a predominant one can go a long way toward pulsing relative strangers and knowing how best to communicate with them.

WHEN THEY'VE PULSED YOU WRONG

While you're reading signals from other people, they're reading signals from you. So it's important to know what signals you send. How do people see you? What value do they place on your time? Are they quick or slow to upset you? Do they take you for granted? These are only a few questions, but they're a good start.

Jennifer Nathan, California entrepreneur, is one of many, many women who are asked to do things for other people for free. There is an unstated expectation that women will do what you want for less money, and this used to happen to me when I was asked to speak at events. You have to know your worth or all of the men there will be making twice as much as you for the same or less time onstage, and you'll also be meeting with people afterward. Nathan was asked by someone she did not know well to read and critique her new website. She asked Nathan to provide a "peer review," which Nathan took to mean work for free. Then the person also gave Nathan a deadline; she needed the free review soon. Nathan didn't refuse. Instead, she offered to think about it. "I wanted to be able to decide whether I could do this or should perhaps offer to do one page because I didn't want to say no outright. And I wanted to assess if this was indeed for free. Maybe that was an assumption," Nathan told me. "After all," she said, "in the absence of information, people make up their own." And she didn't want to do that. She wanted to determine, too, if this was something she should do to avoid others hearing that she would not even help out someone who needed it.

Nathan and I talked about how women so often give away their talents. She knew that. I knew that. But I also understood her desire not to shut this woman down without considering whether this was one favor that might require less effort than she initially perceived. But as a rule, women should be very wary of their tendency to give to those who are going to simply take.

I love Bob Cialdini's take on this, for both men and women. In his book *Influence*,[5] Cialdini writes of scarcity, specifically that if what you have to offer is perceived as being scarce, it's of greater value. So giving it away cheapens it. Cialdini recommends when doing a favor for someone that you make clear to them that some degree of reciprocity is expected in the near or perhaps distant future. Otherwise they'll pulse you as an easy mark. And that's never good.

He recommends that when someone expresses appreciation you consider saying something like this:

"You're very welcome. You'd do the same for me, I'm sure."

This response sets the parameters of a favor. It lets the person know in a very civil way that you are pleased to help them but that sometime in the future they may be called upon to do something for you. Additionally, it suggests, without specifying, that you don't customarily give away things and that the other person should think next time before asking. People who do favors for whoever asks and who reply to thanks with, "It's no trouble at all"—after spending hours helping someone—might as well wear a sign on their forehead reading: "Ask me. I don't expect anything in return."

It's a fun phrase for a T-shirt, but short of that it's useless. People don't respect those who are always available, but most are more than willing to take what such people provide without a thought of a return favor. If you are a person who gives too much away for nothing in return, it's time to change. You need to start sending out signals that you are no longer available to any and all people wanting you to do things for them. You are busy, your time is valuable, and it's high time they realized it.

How do you send such signals? It's best to begin with small ones rather than have people think you suddenly got grumpy or that something is terribly wrong with you today. Then they simply wait around for you to come back to who you were. Small signals can be expressed in words or gestures:

"That sounds like something I'd like to do, but not this time."

People may look oddly at you if they aren't used to such comments, but the key is to stay with the new plan. If they ask,"What's gotten into you?" you might reply, "I've put myself on a schedule in order to complete my novel." Now, if you're not planning to write a novel or don't want to sound smug, just substitute some other important goal.

Returning to the situation Jennifer Nathan faced, how might she refuse to do a favor for which she is unlikely to receive anything in return? Some women would simply say no. In fact, I've met many who know their worth. But Nathan also works in a small network, and there is some benefit to letting people down easily. Her idea of perhaps critiquing one page is not a bad one. But better would be if she could think of something that this person could also do for her. Better still would be acknowledging that she is willing to help to some extent because the requester is new and probably young. Given the value of her time, she could ask that this person include on her website a link to Nathan's site, and maybe a brief bio; or she might simply decline to help because her schedule doesn't permit it. Here are some other options for what she might say:

"I'll gladly do *x* if you'll be so kind as to do *y* for me."

"I can help you this time, but let's keep that between us."

"If you can work with my schedule, I may be able to help."

"I'm tied up for weeks, so let's revisit this after that."

"Such things always look easy, but I find they take time I can't afford."

"I'm not the person for this. If I were, I'd say so. You need an expert."

"I don't commit unless I can do things well, so it's better for you if I decline."

These are relatively civil ways of saying no, or at least "not now." There are many more ways, and once you get the hang of it people are less likely to expect you to do their work for them. As a professor, I learned that once students found out that I was publishing books, speaking, consulting, counseling, and writing grant proposals, they treated my time as valuable. They came to my office prepared to explain, as quickly and as clearly as they could, what they needed. The signals I was inadvertently sending said: "I'm busy." In fact, it got to the point where some would apologize for interrupting me when I was working in my office. But I wanted them to come in, especially during office hours. So I made sure they knew I was available. I didn't however, say, "Oh, don't be silly, call me or drop by anytime." That would have sent an entirely different set of signals, and much of my research, writing, and publishing—not to mention the students themselves—would likely have been shortchanged on account of that frittering away of time.

Perhaps the most important point to take away from this section is that while you're pulsing someone, they're pulsing you. Since you're at least 75 percent responsible for how you're treated, you have to watch and listen to see if they're getting it right. If they're relying on assumptions about you due to size, age, appearance, what you've said so far, and so on, you need to correct them. Otherwise, you're boxed in where you don't want to be.

CHAPTER TEN

Assessing the Situation

Rachel Rongwhey failed to pulse the person when it came to dealing with Marilyn, but she also failed to assess the situation. She had only been working at Wastenot for three months. That's too early to take on someone in anger if it's at all avoidable. When you're new to a job, there is much to learn that's easily observable, and much more that isn't. A lot of rules at work are subliminal. You only come to know what they are by seeing others break them, or by breaking them yourself. So to think that three months at a new job, no matter how many years of experience she'd gained elsewhere, was sufficient for Rachel to act as she did was naïve.

She didn't fully consider the status difference and focused instead on her own need to be right. Marilyn was her boss. There is, like it or not, a certain line that especially a new employee doesn't cross with a superior at work. In some companies that line barely exists, but at most it quickly shows itself in the expression on the offended person's face when you come too close to it.

By not assessing the situation effectively before deciding how to respond, Rachel didn't even notice that she may have indeed had an argument in her favor that might have caused Marilyn to feel bad and attempt to reciprocate in a positive way. Rachel might have used the status aspect of her situation—being a new employee—to justify how shocked she was at Marilyn's harsh tone.

The use of e-mail could have been a focus, too. The e-mail was sent just before Marilyn left for home. Rachel muttered about how Marilyn knew sending it at that late hour would prevent resolving the problem until the next day. Rachel believed, too, that Marilyn wanted her to have to deal with the insult late into the evening. To Rachel, this was a breach of civility. The meeting had been earlier in the afternoon, so Marilyn had time to walk over to Rachel's office to discuss her concerns. The memo was an insult to Rachel and also, it seemed, the possible beginning of a paper trail.

Rachel was probably right about one thing at least. Marilyn's use of an end-of-day e-mail to convey bad news wasn't professional. It didn't suit the way things are usually done at Wastenot, especially when it came to wasting Rachel's time worrying about and dealing with it. But Rachel confused a situational error with an intentional personal affront.

Viewing the events in this way certainly limited Rachel's options. She could have framed it as first and foremost a breach of company etiquette, or as something outside what would be expected of a manager with whom Rachel had not had any significant problems in the past. Then she might have asked a question to assess if her other concerns were legitimate. Once in Marilyn's office, she might have responded to the e-mail debacle as follows:

Marilyn: Rachel, you look upset about something. Is it the memo?
Rachel: The memo bothered me, Marilyn. But it was more the process involved in sending it.
Marilyn: What do you mean?
Rachel: Sending it so late in the day left me no opportunity to reply until the next day, which meant that I ended up worrying about it most of last night. At Wastenot, that's a serious waste of valuable time. Had you spoken to me, we could have resolved the whole thing quickly.

Marilyn: I was in such a rush. It wasn't until I was in my car and had picked up Billy early because he wasn't feeling well that I thought about how I'd handled that.

Rachel: I can see why you would have been distracted. Is he feeling better now?

Marilyn: Yes. Thank you. And you won't be getting any more late-day memos, Rachel. In fact, I do have high regard for you, and the words I used didn't convey that. I should have thought longer about what to say and how to say it.

Rachel: Do you have time at lunch to deal with where we go from here?

Marilyn: Absolutely. Let's do that.

THE BEAUTY OF A PROCESS COMEBACK

A process comeback—pointing out an error in how an issue is being approached—is often the best way to start a discussion about something that has transpired and made one or more people uncomfortable. It often works beautifully because it distances the person from the error. What might have been viewed as an intentional attack (because of timing or how it was conveyed) can be framed as a violation of normal practice, as an action that is not conducive to promoting company goals, or as an obstacle to maintaining good working relationships. Instead of commenting on what someone said, using a process comeback involves saying something like, *"I think we've gone off course here"* or *"The cart is going before the horse in this discussion. We haven't defined the problem before deciding how to deal with it."*

Taking a process approach does not mean that once the comeback has been stated—and hopefully executed effectively—specific personal aspects of the situation can't be addressed. But they are then presented as secondary issues. Rachel Rongwhey could have addressed process with Marilyn as in the example above. Then, later, perhaps at lunch, she might have discussed her personal reactions to Marilyn's words. But again, she'd want to do this only if the issue hadn't been fully resolved earlier. And she wouldn't need to go over every issue on her mind but instead could talk briefly with Marilyn about ways to communicate with each other in the future when problems arise.

The next time you encounter someone in a senior position saying or doing something that could be seen as a procedural error, consider positioning your comeback to address that. It can be very effective. Once someone notices that an error they made is due to poor process, they are at liberty to become less defensive, since process errors occur often at work. Then you can address anything you see as personal, if that is still important. And if you do so by saying, "There's just one more thing, and it's easily fixed . . ." before addressing the personal issue, it frames it as secondary and therefore less of an offense.

ALL COMEBACKS ARE SITUATION-SPECIFIC

As we've already discussed, it doesn't pay to simply memorize a bunch of comebacks and toss them out whenever the spirit moves you. There are many aspects of situations to consider before choosing and employing a comeback. Sometimes this has to be done quickly. But it has to be done. In the following pages, we're going to share a few examples that demonstrate how situation influences choices.

When You've Been Insulted

What would you do if you went to a dinner with friends and, after you said something about your job, the host turned to everyone at the table and said, "Didn't I tell you she'd be talking about work within five minutes?" This actually happened to a friend. And she was very insulted.

On this occasion, not only were the words insulting, but so too was the dismissive way in which they were presented. The goal was not to help change the subject but to humiliate the person speaking. That's just plain rude.

The woman who told me this story was struck speechless. She is rarely so. In fact, she is normally quick on her feet. But this was one blow that she never saw coming. Furthermore, it had an element of truth to it, in terms of how much she likes to talk about her work. This made the comment an insult to her as person, rather than some random comment the host might have made. Derogatory comments with a slight element of truth to them can certainly hurt. And they often leave their targets unable to respond, as they're busy trying to figure out the motive of the person deriving such pleasure from their discomfort or displeasure. It's a tough spot to be in.

What would you say in reply? One of these might be a good option:

"I'm excited about what I do. As are you." Perhaps add a smile and move on by saying, "Let me just wrap up my earlier story."

"You mean I actually went five minutes before doing that? I'll have to work on it."

"Well, you're certainly the type of host that makes people want to visit again."

As the saying goes, the best defense is a good offense. The second option above is the most mild. The first and third can be, if said humorously. You have to decide with comebacks whether you want to clearly make your point but also to some extent be sure to save the face of the person to whom you're speaking. Here are a few more options, each with a slight edge:

"Are you this kind to all your guests?"

"I suppose you think that ten-minute talk on golf you gave yesterday was spellbinding for the rest of us."

Of course, if you don't want the evening ruined, you can add a smile to any of the above comebacks. Or, if you're seated next to the offending person, you can place your hand on his back as do buddies engaged in verbal sparring.

One thing you shouldn't do in response to a public insult is brag about what you do right or come across as indignantly arrogant. "If I were as limited with words as you are, I'd be saying less too," may be fun to say, but it toots your horn to silence the offender. Know-it-alls and braggarts don't win arguments, advises Los Angeles attorney Robert Mayer, author of *How to Win Any Argument.* Or as Mayer puts it so well: "Don't accept your dog's admiration as conclusive evidence that you're wonderful."[1] This doesn't mean you can't come across as knowledgeable, professional, and serious about your work, but "there's a difference between being serious about what you do and serious about who you are. The former is appreciated, the latter is not."[2]

When someone puts you down, try one of these confident, but not self-important, responses:

"I could respond to that, but you've done yourself enough damage already."

"If you had it to do over, would you say that again?"

"Do you regularly insult people you hardly know?"

"I'm wondering here whether you actually said what I think I heard."

"Fortunately for you, I'm speechless."

"I could say what I'm thinking, but leaving it to the imagination works, too."

"You're certainly not a comedian."

"I'll bet you were up all night thinking of that one."

"This time we could pretend you didn't say that."

"I see why you might *think* that, but I see no excuse for your *saying* it."

"Do you want to apologize now or later? Whatever suits you."

"That comment wasn't at all like you."

"You don't think that insult was a bit over the top?"

"This is when most people would respond in kind."

"This reminds me of Eleanor Roosevelt's observation: 'Great minds discuss ideas, average minds discuss events, small minds discuss people.'"

None of the above is vicious; some are even gracious ways of helping the source reconsider his or her words. As I've stressed throughout, aggressive retorts should be used sparingly because they often betray a lack of couth or an absence of wittiness. But on occasion people need to be severely brought up short.

When You Insult Someone

On the other hand, we shouldn't leave this section before discussing what to do when it was you who did the insulting. There are times when what seems mildly offensive to one person is taken as a serious insult by another. A former student in my international M.B.A. communication class who is now very successful in high-tech told me of one he'll always remember.

*Long story short, in a presentation at my former company, I used the familiar form of "you" (*du *in German) instead of the polite form (*Sie*) for a vice president, an older corporate gentleman who demanded respect. Worse, I did it in front of a crowd. Worse, I combined what I said with the way I said it: "Verstehst du?" ("Do you understand?"). What I meant to say was "Get it?" but it came out more like "You stupid child, you don't understand anything." Worse, I didn't realize my mistake until after I saw his angry red face, and by then the moment for public apology had come and gone. Nobody laughed. The presentation was over. I had to apologize individually, to every single person, over and over.*

This was an accidental offense, you might say. Surely, you're likely thinking, the German hosts forgave him. Well, they did, just not for a while. And they didn't forget it. The problem was largely one of context. A series of slight and not so slight offenses together moved along the offense-insult continuum to the insult side. But it was the public nature of the mistakes that made them particularly problematic. There is an expectation that those doing business at a high level, which can include speaking a foreign language without an interpreter, are sufficiently fluent to avoid offensive remarks. So, in this situation, what might have been allowed to pass were the presenter speaking to a group of youthful peers was received as quite a serious affront.

Of course, you don't even have to cross cultures at work to get yourself in trouble. So you need to be very sensitive to situational cues. If you do make a mistake, apologies expressed sincerely are usually the best option. Insisting that everyone misinterpreted your words or that you were trying your best is not enough. It usually generates further anger or makes people more upset. Apologies are difficult for many people, but necessary in life because we all make mistakes.

When to Let It Go

Then there are situations where a response just isn't necessary. Again, reading the situation is critical.

Alicia Alan, a California-based business consultant, told me of a situation she finds annoying. A woman with whom she meets regularly as part of an association to which they both belong has the habit of calling her "honey."

"What do I say to make her stop?" she asked me. "I know what I'd do if she were a man, but this is different. She is just one of those people who is bubbly and hugs people and calls them 'honey.' But I don't like it."

Now, I can see why this is annoying, but is this a situation that really needs to be fixed? I put that question to Alan. She paused.

"That's a good question."

"How often do you see her?" I asked.

"Not often," she told me.

"And does she do this just to you?"

"No," was the reply.

185

"Does she introduce you this way or embarrass you professionally by hugging you and referring to you as 'honey' in the middle of business discussions?"

Again, no.

"Then I'd let this one go," I told her. This was a friendly person with no ulterior motive who likes people and has learned, likely in her youth, to be effusive. Some annoying behaviors simply do not lend themselves to correction—even to politically sensitive correction. When an occurrence is rare, when the downside of letting the behavior continue is minimal, and when correction may damage or ruin an otherwise good relationship, it's best to let the annoyance pass, to reframe it as a quirk and get on with more important issues.

I did suggest, however, that if things got worse Alan could say, *"Mary, I like you a lot but I'm just not the 'honey' type,"* or tell her before others join you, *"Tonight, let's hold the 'honey' greeting. You're a warm person but some of these people aren't."* If Mary "gets it," she may not use "honey" to refer to Alan on subsequent occasions.

Sometimes You Have to Poke the Bear

That's what Tim West did when dealing with a bully who just wouldn't stop humiliating and shouting at people in his department. This is how he described the situation:

Our hospital had major financial difficulties that eventually resulted in filing for Chapter 11 protection. Most of upper management and many employees were laid off by a consulting group hired by the board of directors. The consulting group's interim CEO and CFO were quite competent and professional.

Unfortunately the interim COO was your basic bully and treated the department VPs and managers in a very demeaning manner. Our weekly management team meetings were essentially a one-way communication. The managers were afraid to share any opinions contrary to the interim COO's. (Well, except for me—I was described by my peers as "poking the bear.")

After experiencing this behavior for a few meetings I decided to make a symbolic statement. I wore a military helmet to the meeting and when the interim COO asked me why I was wearing the helmet I said, "These meetings get pretty rough at times and I felt I needed the protection." As the meeting proceeded I offered the helmet to other management team members [who were] taking abuse.

Wearing a helmet was a clever way of dealing with this COO. But West didn't do it without considering the situation. As he told me, one of his colleagues was concerned about him taking this COO on. He told West right after the helmet comeback that it was risky. This didn't faze West. He believed someone had to stop the guy and he was not only up to the task but also confident that it was the best move, given the situation. "Unlike the colleague who was worried," West told me, "I didn't have a kid in college depending on me. I was thinking of moving on anyway. And it was important to the people there that someone stop the ugly way this guy was treating everyone." West assessed the situation and decided "poking the bear" was better than letting him tear people apart every day. And so he wore his helmet.

"Surprisingly, I worked there for quite some time after that," West said. No one else had stood up to this COO, and he probably worried that firing West would make him look even worse. But West hadn't considered that. It turned out to be a windfall.

Later on, this same bully used a different surprise tactic at another meeting. West explained:

The interim COO . . . was berating us for not knowing our expenses and revenue. He proudly shook at us a computer report he obtained from our hospital information system and told us this is the report we should use to assess our revenue and expenses. Before he could pass the report out for our examination I pulled the same report from my notebook and said to him, "Are you talking about this report?"

He examined my report, which also had my notes analyzing the expense variances, and suddenly had nothing to say. I also pointed out that the revenue data is gross charges and had nothing to do with the actual revenue information he was seeking.

This probably did not have a great impact on our interim COO's behavior, but I think the managers appreciated that the bully was silenced at least for a short time.

The hospital eventually went into Chapter 11 and my consulting contract was terminated (which I expected and suggested to the COO several months before, to save expenses). A few weeks later I communicated with the interim COO's consulting company and expressed my opinions—most very positive except for the interim COO's behavior. I understand that the interim COO began to temper his behavior.

Not everyone could do this and have it work to their advantage when dealing with a bully. But as this organization became more political, reactions that might seem bizarre in normal circumstances actually proved to be quite functional. They threw the COO off balance.

Here is another case where understanding that a specific situation is leading to public humiliation makes an unusual response necessary. Phyllis Henry, longtime registered nurse and new hospital board member when I met her, faced a situation similar to one all of us confront at one time or another—where you simply cannot let someone walk all over you to make his point. She recounted what happened at one directors' meeting:

I was talking about how effective technology can be in the medical setting. Specifically, I was discussing with the rest of the board the value of offsite advice, and of experts in other parts of the country or world having input via technology into a surgical procedure.

Out of nowhere this board member I didn't even know said loudly and with a derogatory tone, "Oh, please! When is the last time you were ever at a patient's bedside?"

You could hear a pin drop in the room.

I'm usually able to do quick checks and say the right thing, but this was out of line and I was new to the board. I turned to him and said, "Excuse me, I'm a nurse. You obviously don't know what I do. We're going to have to talk about this later."

I was so angry that I needed to make that point, but I wasn't going to fight it out with him on the spot. After the meeting he half apologized. But I didn't let it go, because I will be working with him in the future. I need to know if this was a whipping-girl thing or a jackass thing. I'll see him again in two weeks and I'll find out.

By establishing her credibility, and diminishing his for failing to check his assumptions, and all in two or three short sentences, Henry displayed what we might call a truly adept "boardside manner." The situation warranted her strong response. Actually, it was highly professional of Henry to keep the entire potential conflict from playing out in the board meeting itself. The other directors may all know this man is difficult, or at least that he commonly speaks before he thinks, but she needed more information before either attacking him or letting him off the hook—and so her decision to put off the actual confrontation until after the meeting was an excellent move.

When I talked with her she was considering what she would say to him when she expected they would meet again in two weeks' time. Here is one possible reply she mentioned:

What's the deal, Jake? I respect you as a clinician. So I'm wondering why you don't respect me as a clinician.

It was off the top of her head, and by the time she decides what to say to him it likely won't be this one. Why? Because it would be asking for respect from a person who has shown her disrespect. Besides, even if he didn't know she was a nurse—which is doubtful, since board members usually know such things about new directors—then it wasn't a lack of respect for her work but rather a failure to pay the respect due a fellow board member. Indeed, she shouldn't ask him for anything at all. She should simply let him know that what he said to her must not happen again. You don't achieve that by asking a disrespectful person for respect; you insist that they change their ways.

Henry might say, *"Jake, you came way out of left field at that board meeting. The next time you want to make a point when you're angry, make sure you do it at your own expense, not mine."* If that's not her style, she might say, *"Let's put this behind us for the sake of the hospital. But think hard before you attempt to demean what I have to say. The next time I won't be so polite."* Or, as another, less direct, alternative, she might say: *"When you disagree with me, Jake, try being civil and we'll be fine."* Or, perhaps most effectively, she might say: *"I went easy on you, which is more than you can say. But be clear on this: I only do that once."*

That last one can be useful on a lot of contentious occasions. So you might want to write it down and memorize it.

LEARN THE TABOOS

Organizations and individuals usually harbor forbidden topics or have pet peeves about certain ways people act. Assessing a situation can also involve noting what topics or approaches are taboo.

Overstating your ability may be a quick way to have people dislike you in a company or in a division where that kind of thing is just not done. Acting like a know-it-all could work in the same negative way, as we've discussed. *I can't stand ass-kissers and yes-people,* a successful senior member of a temporary-employment agency told me, *"and people who don't speak up when they know something isn't going to work."* Stealing other people's ideas is something else she can't abide. People who do these things land on her bad side for a long time. If you work for her and don't know about these taboos, you're likely to get on her wrong side, and stay there.

She herself once worked for a boss who mistook any possessive actions for a desire to take control. He had no patience with keeping good ideas close to the vest or talking about "I" instead of "we." She learned the hard way while working for him not to imply ownership of ideas or ways of doing things, and not to take credit for them unless the boss suggests you deserve to do so.

Some people hate anything that sounds like conflict, even if it isn't. If you're not aware of that particular pet peeve, you're bound to use a comeback that looks good on paper or in your head but then falls like a lead balloon.

A FOOL'S PARADISE

Assessing the situation can also be about suffering fools when absolutely necessary. Personally, I'm not inclined toward this for more than short periods of time, and only on rare occasions, but you will find, with experience, that some fools may need to be tolerated, especially if the end is in sight. Simon Arnold, an engineering firm executive, described one such situation to me.

"The culture of this company tolerates fools for years," Arnold explained. "One guy wasn't going be fired, so you had to live with him. He was a complete ass, but as a finance guy he was very good. He was my fellow VP and also CFO of our business unit, but he had no socially redeeming characteristics. In fact, he was the worst ass I ever encountered in my business career, and that is saying something."

Arnold determined that there was no use trying to come up with a clever comeback when dealing with this guy. He was always making enemies all by himself, so it wasn't a case where Arnold needed to make sure he looked better. When everyone knows the other guy is vicious yet the culture promotes him nonetheless, there's little to be gained by giving him the fight he clearly seeks. Arnold described one incident:

He had been put in charge of Asian operations. At the time, Asian HQ was in Hong Kong, which was very expensive, and so he moved Asian HQ to our offices in Tokyo. He kicked the Japanese country manager out of the GM's office so he could have it. Great way to make friends and influence people. He was great at provoking verbal fistfights. At one of our off-site business strategy meetings, in front of everyone, he said that I was "worthless" and had not done anything useful for the company in years. The room got so quiet that you could hear the proverbial pin drop. He wanted me to respond in anger, to help him escalate the insult. Instead, I rose from my chair slowly and walked over to the window, as if he didn't exist. I stayed there until one of my colleagues restarted the conversation on another topic.

You see, everyone knew he was a jerk. He also regularly verbally assaulted my marketing colleague. But he was so good with the numbers and analysis of acquisition targets that he was tolerated. None of us could avoid him because we were all part of the same executive team, but he was not someone to seek out.

He wasn't so much a political animal as just an animal. He

*was always on the offensive, damaging somebody, and nobody
wanted it to be them.*

Knowing Arnold, if he didn't have to put up with someone like
this, he wouldn't have, but he read the situation, noted how long it
would take for the offending party to retire, and stayed out of his
way as much as possible. There are some people who are just there to
stay, even if they are "animals."

You have to ask yourself if it's worth it to go up against them, if
it might not be more irksome to them if you simply didn't respond.
Often it's better to go around them as much as possible. A lot depends on how much of a fool you're suffering and whether that fool
is out to get you. If it's truly a matter of jeopardizing your career,
violating your code, or letting someone else get burned, then you
might have to take such people on. Even if you win, a culture like
the one Arnold worked in often promotes such people out of the
problem they're creating. It's called upward failure.

To close the chapter, here's some more advice for dealing with a
difficult, insulting person:

- **Simply walk away slowly.**
- **Change the subject of discussion, as if the person attacking
  you doesn't exist.**
- **Use the attacker's own words to annoy him. Arnold might
  have turned to another person and said,** *"Speaking of 'worthless,' Al, let's look at the direction of today's meeting."*
- **Say:** *"There's something déjà vu about this conversation—as if
  most of us have been before where I stand now. Let's move on."*
- **Say:** *"Funny how 'worthless' to one person is 'promising' to another."*
- **Say:** *"I'll be over here. When the conversation turns civil again,
  would one of you let me know?"*

Next time you're about to employ a comeback, be sure not to take Rachel Rongwhey's approach. Do some observing. Consider how public the situation is, how significant the offense or insult, whether this person will ever change, whether it's worth your getting upset, and the long- and short-term advantages of saying what's on your mind.

CHAPTER ELEVEN

Ten Questions to Ask Yourself

What we've discussed so far is a lot of information to keep in mind when something goes wrong in a relationship at work. In chapter 6 we took a shortcut approach with the R-List. Now let's consolidate some of what's been written into a set of ten key questions that will determine the best way for you to select a comeback so that you'll rarely if ever need to say, "I wish I'd said . . ." again. Think of them as another tool, like the R-List, also to be kept in your desk drawer for quick reference. After using them for a while, these questions will pop into your mind in a matter of seconds, and you'll be able to respond more effectively on your feet.

1. HOW MUCH DO YOU CARE ABOUT THIS RELATIONSHIP?

As we've discussed, you should become comfortable using a range of comebacks that you select according to whether you must maintain a relationship for professional reasons, you desire to maintain it for personal reasons, or there's no need to maintain the relationship at all. A teasing comment from a good friend might warrant your saying, with feigned annoyance, *"Have you quite finished?"* whereas an avid adversary may deserve the slightly above-threshold response

"Are you like this on a regular basis or can we plan on this being a unique experience?" Sometimes the best comeback is an admission—*"You're quite right. I stand corrected."* At other times, it may be wise to not give ground but nevertheless acknowledge the other person's point has some validity: *"You've obviously done your homework"* or *"I can see where you're coming from."* Whatever the situation, I have a rule: If you can respond without wounding the relationship or the other person's ego, choose the comeback that does so.

A senior executive I coached for a few years may have needed my help in some areas, but with regard to understanding the value of maintaining relationships she was very skilled. This is a situation she shared with me.

"Take the high road" is a phrase I use a lot with people I work closely with, particularly when they come to me with challenges regarding our sister division. While overall the relationship has improved, we are still faced with regular challenges regarding working effectively and being able to trust them. At times they seem to try and put a wedge between us and do not typically partner with us but rather against us.

Many of the original partners who started the company have a more direct line and years of history with the chairman. They seem to influence him a lot and bend his ear often. Recently one of these partners visited one of our remote locations. She left with the impression that the office was "dead." She felt there was no activity and little synergy. She told the chairman this and he immediately reacted by storming into my office and telling me to visit the location myself in the next week.

My initial reaction was to defend and tell him reasons why she may have gotten the "dead" impression. Half the staff was in training, for example. I wanted to call her right away and defend myself.

Instead, I thought to take the high road. I would follow my chairman's instruction. I called him later that day to let him know I had called the partner and was seeking additional impressions. I promised to keep him posted. And I did the same with her. She was very open with me and more positive than I expected. She did not become defensive because of the way I approached her. Even though I was angry that she hadn't come to me first, that wasn't as important as maintaining the relationship. She was very positive about the group and their potential level of commitment. The situation was a turning point with her. She tends to be cold and always points fingers. This time she felt like we were a team. She now trusts me more, and she is not quick to trust.

In *The Secret Handshake* I wrote that people who get ahead are usually those who make others feel good about having them around. It's great to be quick-witted, but if you're always using that talent to pull the rug out from under people, you're going to make a lot of enemies.

As a sports equipment company senior executive told me, "You always have to ask yourself what good is going to come of this." You might get anger off your chest, and pay for it the rest of your career.

A business development executive told me, "I largely make people look good." This wasn't always her modus operandi, though; she had to learn to do it. Indeed, she told me about how contagious she had once found it to work for a "screamer." She'd started screaming at people too. "It took me a fifteen-month sabbatical to change around," she told me.

That doesn't mean she always avoids stepping on toes. In fact, in a fast-paced company, that is bound to happen. "I don't have time to be the queen of collaboration," she explained, but added that she'd rather teach fourth grade (which she knew she wouldn't be good at) than go around screaming or berating people like another boss whom she had tolerated for two years.

We're all different, and sometimes it's difficult to avoid being provoked to anger. But we're all works in progress and there is no such thing as a perfect person or someone who always communicates with perfect clarity. If you care about a relationship, for whatever reason—even just to be civil—why not give yourself and other people a break by pausing to reflect before responding? Then if you must be direct, you'll know it was not because of a knee-jerk reaction.

2. TO WHAT EXTENT IS THE OFFENSE PURPOSEFUL?

This bears repeating and reviewing. We've mentioned it throughout the book because it is so important to how you interpret what other people say and do and thus determine how you should respond. People push past each other in a rush, sneeze too close to others, get grumpy at stop signs, or blurt out something less than complimentary. But if we spend our days reacting strongly to such offenses, we have little energy left for dealing with real insults.

It's important to prioritize. Essentially you ask yourself: "How close to my threshold of tolerance has this person transgressed?" Use the Insult/Intent continuums in chapter 3, and when in doubt, ask the person:

"Did you mean to insult me just then?"

This gives them a chance to reflect on their questionable behavior and perhaps say something to help bring the relationship back to a firmer foundation—what we have called "giving them a chance to do the right thing."

But if the action in question is clearly a purposeful insult, that's a different story. Let's say you're about to enter a meeting and you run an idea past your colleague, Tim. He likes it but thinks it needs work, so at the meeting you hesitate to introduce it. But just as the meeting is about to end, he suggests it himself and grabs all the credit. It's highly unlikely that this is an accidental offense. Even if you think he might say, *"The idea I just introduced may have been somewhat like yours but not much,"* you need to act. What might you say? Here's one possible scenario:

You: When I gave you that idea before the meeting we decided it wasn't ready to introduce.
Tim: I meant to mention your input.
You: There's a lot more to this idea, so I'll pick up where Tim left off when we meet tomorrow.
Tim: I got a little overenthusiastic about your idea and shouldn't have blurted it out like that.
You: That happens. We can pick up where we left off with it when we all meet tomorrow.

Here you're letting him off the hook, but because of your directness, people in the room already know that Tim, no matter his reason, stole your idea, and they're not likely to forget that. He's unlikely to be doing it again soon. Sure, you could talk with him after the meeting. He may be the type of person who deserves that gift. But if this idea is an important one and stealing it was a major affront to you, then you should at least say, "When I told you that idea before the meeting, Tim, we'd decided not to introduce it yet. It may have been premature to do so today. So let's make time at the next meeting to discuss its development." This is a kinder approach and makes the point. It could, however, come across as sour grapes. To avoid this, the tone of delivery and focus would have to be one of professional concern for a good idea rather than personal betrayal. Another option, "I've been working on that idea for weeks, and shared it with Tim. He obviously liked it. But it needs more development, so let's save some time at the next meeting to revisit it."

3. DID YOU CONTRIBUTE? DO YOU OWN PART OF THE PROBLEM?

If we think back to the discussion on unwanted repetitive episodes (URPs), it's clear that much of what we say and do during each day is influenced by how we've communicated in the past with people. We also must recognize that it isn't always the other person who is responsible for a communication problem. When you find yourself in an URP or in a situation where a person you've never met before is acting as if she doesn't like you, you have to ask yourself: *To what extent am I contributing to this?"* Some people formulate attributions very quickly and decide whether they like people or not within seconds. If you've ever been on the receiving end of such hasty decisions, you know that it can cause arguments unless one or the other person takes note of what has occurred and attempts to reconstruct things right away. Here is one way to deal with a person who is responding to you in a negative way:

> *Occasionally I rub people the wrong way with my brusqueness. It's a habit I picked up in my previous workplace. Perhaps that happened here, as I seem to be making you uncomfortable.*

The other person has some choices here. He or she can say, *"Oh, no. I admire directness."* If something like this is said, then both you and she have taken note of how you're communicating and can go forward in a more positive way. However, if instead, he or she says, *"You're awfully abrupt,"* you're at a choice point. If the goal of reaching some kind of agreement is more important than your seeming angelic, I'd go with, *"So you noticed that, too,"* and then, smiling,

"Well, then let's start over and I'll keep that adorable side of myself in check."

Some people just don't see the point of doing this. They prefer to be right. Or they want to make sure the other person knows that he or she is part of the problem. But the question here is: Why? If the relationship is important to the goal, why not say something like this?

> "Let's back up. You and I met here because we want the same thing. We may have different ways of going about it—different styles, for sure—but that's insignificant compared to what we both want out of this."

This doesn't put the blame on anyone. It refocuses on the problem or issue at hand. It puts both of you in the same boat, so to speak. And it usually gives people a chance to rethink what matters and how their personal style might be getting in the way. One other option might be:

> "There is something going on that has little to do with you and me. Am I right? Is there some reason why we're slipping into a contentious discussion over something we both care about?"

4. IS YOUR CREDIBILITY—OR SOMETHING ELSE VALUABLE TO YOU—ON THE LINE?

I was trained in a field of study in which ripping presenters to shreds at conferences was a part of the culture. Even as a graduate student, after preparing countless hours for a conference talk, my coauthors and I were often treated to senior professors standing up to tell the audience about all the things that were wrong both with the research and with us. It was a boot camp for communication scientists. And I did get some good training out of it.

Fortunately, I'd been a debater in my undergraduate years, and attacks of this nature often brought out the best in me. I'd often feel an initial terror, and then, as the opposition went on, I'd find in his comments a number and range of errors. Then I would graciously (when possible) note what he'd said that had merit—and give him back in spades what he had given me where he was wrong. Usually the critic would respect a good verbal battle if we knew what we were talking about. And that is partly how I, and others like me, moved forward in the field of communication. When our credibility was on the line, we fired back—and with sufficient evidence and confidence to make future attackers think twice before taking us on again.

We all have experiences like that in our careers, and even in our personal lives. Some situations are critical to your career or your self-esteem. We've put a good deal of emphasis in this book on ways to say things that don't cause others to lose face. But when they've attempted to scorch the earth with your reputation, it's time to give back as good as you got.

5. DID THE PERSON ATTACKING YOU DO ENOUGH DAMAGE TO HIMSELF?

Remember this discussion from earlier in the book? If you really listen carefully, often you'll notice that the person who just tried to make you look bad is sinking his own boat in the process. There may be no need for you to shoot further holes in it; doing so may only make you look bad. In such situations, your best response is often silence and a pensive look, perhaps with squinted eyes, as if wondering whether he or she has really said what you heard. Or you could just allow yourself a slight shake of the head before changing the subject. How do you know, though, when a person has sabotaged himself in an attempt to damage you?

Perhaps you, like I, have witnessed someone who should be old enough to know better bullying a junior colleague. Perhaps the young person says something that most people in the room know isn't a subject that should be brought up, and the senior manager proceeds to rip into him. Remember Tim West wearing a helmet to a meeting to get a bully COO to stop berating people?

Perhaps you've sat in on a meeting with a senior executive team where the CEO has showered praise on his favorite managers and belittled the other ones. When the belittled felt compelled to defend themselves, the CEO became more angry. Others in the room may have looked down at their shoes. I was invited by a CEO like this to fix his people. He wanted me around to tell him why things weren't going the way he wanted and who was to blame.

"Sometimes you're a bully," I told him. "People look to you for leadership and often you attack them. So they spend much of their time dodging your anger." That didn't sit too well with him, but I'd warned him at the start of my consulting that he'd hear what I thought, not what he wanted me to say. I told him he was his worst enemy when he behaved like a jaguar taking on a kitten. Respect doesn't accrue to those who, instead of educating young people (or, in fact, anyone who works for them), choose to terrorize them. It took time, but this man did eventually mend his ways. Profits rose and people were happier—still wary, but happier.

When dealing with such people it's best to say very little in public. If you're significantly junior to them, talk with someone more senior to learn how you might handle the situation. How did he or she survive? Watch what others say or do when under attack. Consider meeting with the person attacking you and say:

"I know you were disappointed, but your anger made me wonder if there is more to the story. Perhaps something I'm unintentionally doing is rubbing you the wrong way."

If that's too demure for the situation, at the meeting you could say,

"There's bad news in what I just said, but good news, too. We seem to be focused on the bad. So let me restate the positive and the potential it provides."

Make sure you really have some significantly positive things to say. If you do, this approach could reframe things positively for the other person. He may realize that he has already done enough damage to himself by attacking you. And if you're sitting there shaking in your boots or angry, it might be just what's needed. You'll help him look better if he is savvy enough to take you up on your offer.

6. ARE YOU INSERTING YOURSELF INTO THE RESPONSE TOO MUCH?

By this part of the book, you've likely begun taking note of when you insert "I" or "me" into heated discussions, thereby making something that could be handled objectively into something that can't. It's natural to insert ourselves and our feelings into discussions, but with comebacks you have to be sure that's appropriate. If you make an issue about you, the other person might be only too delighted to follow suit. There are few things someone trying to get one past you wants more than to be able to make the discussion about your feelings or to focus on how you see things rather than take an objective look at what is going on.

Keep this in mind, as it's one of the most common mistakes

people make in their comebacks. They feel angry, hurt, duped, or injured—and they say so. That's okay now and then with people who care about how you feel. But it's terrible at work as anything more than an occasional slip. The next time you hear yourself using "I" or "me" when trying to resolve a problem, be sure you want to have the focus become personal. Watch out, too, for discussing your feelings instead of your thoughts or observations. This alone can substantially improve your comeback success.

7. DO THEY KNOW WHAT TO EXPECT OF YOU?

This is a reminder about not being predictable. Since we're creatures of pattern, and expectant of patterns in others, we are surprised when someone who could be angry decides instead to be understanding and helpful. There is tremendous power in the unexpected, so long as we don't overdo it. When little we do is predictable, others become suspicious, considering that we may be manipulative, if not downright strange. They back away. But a modicum of surprise, when least expected, can go a long way.

It's a lot like hearing a person who never swears suddenly say "damn." Everyone looks up. They pay attention because something is different and it makes an impact. You can apply this to your responses in difficult situations. However, it's important to understand what people expect of you.

Early on in my career I had to face the fact that looking young, being a woman, not being large, and having a relatively soft voice was causing people to make assumptions about me that weren't accurate. I worked on my voice, my look, and my ways of responding to the point where, when teaching high school with a "rough" group of kids, I was the only teacher with a quiet study hall. One day, out of frustration, the principal rounded up the study hall teachers for a meeting in his office. But when he passed by my room he said, "You don't need to come. You're the smallest, the youngest, the least scary-looking, but those kids know you mean business."

I achieved this reputation by doing things like refusing to accept rude behavior, and making sure that wise guys or gals I sent to the office actually got there by picking up the phone in my room and informing the vice principal of their impending arrival. But I was helpful to the kids, too, when they were doing their work. Soon, my biggest problem became the formerly troublesome students who made sure that new wise guys mended their ways. One big kid whom I'd sent to the office several times stood up and turned to a new arrival, who, noting my youth, assumed he could do as he pleased. "Don't you talk to Miss Reardon like that," the student bellowed. His eyes scanned the room, letting the others know he meant business, then turned to me, gave me a slight smile, sat back down, and returned to his work. Other former tough guys took note, and helped. Soon there was little required of me to keep the study hall quiet.

If you can come to grips with why people assume things about you that cause them to underestimate or mistreat you, it's possible to make changes. When you find yourself losing ground and failing to make progress with someone, instead of continuing to say the same things over and over again, as if the person were deaf, try a change of tack. This is what a senior government employee did:

One of my direct reports was dragging her feet on sourcing components for an order. This had been happening often because she and a much older director reporting to her didn't get along. I really wanted to tell her to get off her high horse and start working together with him. But after fifteen minutes of unproductive exchange, I decided to try another approach. I suggested that she was the leader in the situation and as the leader she could overcome the director's weaknesses and find new ways to manage him. They still have their differences, and I wish I had the magic words to make them a great team, but sometimes that's just impossible. . . . By getting angry I would have satisfied my short-term need but lost ground on other, long-term issues.

There are no magic words, but some can come close. This senior executive went against his grain by trying something different, something he didn't really want to try going into the situation. It worked and he learned how to stretch his limits, to avoid always doing the same thing and so achieved a different outcome in a situation that otherwise would have continued to damage the division and the company.

The next time people are making assumptions about you that aren't constructive, consider either doing something different or trying to exceed their expectations by impressing them with your preparation and ideas. Rather than get angry, as so many people do about wrong impressions, take a good look at how you act and come across. What should you tweak to alter that impression for the better? After all, you are at least 75 percent responsible for how people treat you, and that means shaping their impressions of you as well.

8. WHAT DOES YOUR GUT INSTINCT TELL YOU? HOW ABOUT THE OTHER PERSON'S BODY LANGUAGE?

It's a good idea here to return to the comeback components model in chapter 7 and to look over that and the questions at the end of the chapter. People who use their gut instinct well have fine-tuned their ability to notice anticipatory clues that alert them that something important is about to happen. Episodic memory may kick in to relate current experience to the past. And the rest of the components, especially in important situations, come together to create a comeback decision that is likely to be effective. If you've become more attuned to such aspects of comebacks, you've done yourself a considerable favor in terms of learning what to say.

But it bears repeating that knowing what to say is just an important first step. People often tell me during coaching sessions, "I'll say *x* to him. That should do it, right?" Maybe. But how a comeback is said is just as important as what is said. Silly as it may sound, there are times when practicing in front of a mirror isn't a bad idea. We often deny our expressional tendencies, but it's better to see them for yourself. Then you're in a position to alter them.

This aspect of comebacks is in part why we demonstrated in chapter 6 that any of the R-List comeback types that tend to be negative can also be positive, based on how the comeback is said. "You're an idiot" sounds negative, but among friends, and with an accompanying smile, it can be funny. So, I would be remiss not to emphasize the importance of facial expression and other body language. You can't convey enthusiasm if you look bored. Telling someone you love their idea doesn't come across that way if your face says otherwise.

The best way we know to improve in this area is to pause the next time people aren't interpreting what you're saying as you intended. Pick one or two trusted people to help you with this. One of my former graduate students who was then CEO of a successful business, shared with the class that some of his employees considered him "slick." He was a pleasant guy, but when he got up in front of a group, his inflections, mannerisms, and facial expressions did make him appear to be a smooth talker. By the end of the semester he knew why, and he had altered his way of presenting himself so that "slick" became a part of his past.

Some people sound superior when they don't intend to come across that way. Others think they're speaking with conviction when you can hardly hear them, or they tend to look away or pause too often. Still others—and in my experience, usually women—smile when they're trying to make a serious point, which certainly undermines an otherwise excellent comeback.

As we mentioned, it's useful to pick up a book on body language if you've never studied this topic. You'll be amazed at the subtle signals we all send all the time, even when we think we're not communicating anything. Some of them we learn from childhood. We don't get a chance to alter the damaging ones unless people along the way advise us how to do so. To be adept at comebacks, you have to know what signals you inadvertently send.

9. ARE YOU SUFFICIENTLY SKILLED TO PULL THIS OFF?

As you've read, we all have our comeback comfort zone. There are things that some people can get away with while others can't—and that's okay. You just have to know where you fit in all this. What are the parameters that at this point in your career you should not cross? What are things others higher up can say and do but you can't as yet? And what skills do they have that you lack?

None of us becomes expert at using comebacks without failing to do so well now and again. Trial and error is the only route, and it's strewn with potholes, for sure. But better to take a stand against how people treat you than to let life—and comebacks—just happen to you. So, tomorrow take things just a bit further, either toward being more direct or less so. Whatever you typically would do, don't do. See how it goes. See how much leeway you get. There's no need to pick a make-or-break situation to try this out. Instead, choose smaller battles so that you can become more confident with comebacks and learn your new limits.

Even if there are no magic words, over time you'll learn that some words tend to work in certain situations better than others. That's part of the goal of reading a book like this. By expanding your repertoire for different types of situations, you'll be able to get past comeback brain freeze and to develop confidence.

10. CAN YOU LIVE WITH THE OUTCOME?

Taking the long view is important in life, but if overdone it can delay action when action is most needed. Somewhere in between is a happy medium. In any case, those who use comebacks effectively are not impulsive, short-term thinkers. They consider the consequences of their actions, often rapidly, on the basis of experience. Even those responding on their feet usually think before doing so. Or they rely on the accumulation of experiences pertaining to the situation at hand and apply what worked well in the past to a similar situation in the present.

Blasting forth with comebacks, even those learned in this book, without consideration of the consequences is usually foolish. There are rare occasions when the offense is so egregious that a strong reaction, no matter the job or career consequences, must be made. Effective communicators have developed ways to prevent themselves from overreacting, and I witnessed a good example of this recently while donating items at a Salvation Army store.

As I waited in the store, a woman asked twice for a price on an item. The clerk replied, "I've been asked many times and I don't have it." She then began to count down from ten. From what I caught of the conversation, her annoyance with the customer seemed unwarranted, but I considered her way of bringing herself back to a calm state to avoid an altercation worthy of note. Had she done it quietly, it would have been admirable. Whatever it takes to keep from saying what is going to cause more problems than the situation warrants is likely a good thing. While counting down from ten aloud could be offensive, taking a deep breath, excusing yourself from a conversation for a few moments, changing the subject, or telling yourself "easy now" are reasonable ways to slow things down a bit.

After that, ask yourself whether the situation calls for an above- or below-threshold response, and then act accordingly. If you do so, you'll be much more likely to achieve your desired outcome.

Keep the ten questions in this chapter in your desk drawer and eventually memorize them; once you have, you'll be ready to assess quickly situations requiring comebacks. If you also keep the R-List firmly in mind and remember some of the comebacks introduced throughout the book that suit you or, even better, stretch you a bit, then being challenged by insults, or in any other way, should become comfortable for you. Such situations are inevitable at work, but the more prepared you are, the better things will go for you. And soon people will be thinking twice before saying something that will generate a comeback from you.

A Few Final Thoughts

As we said in chapter 1, no one is born a comeback expert. In fact, becoming one can be a lifetime avocation, but it's a worthwhile one. There are few things more comforting at work than knowing you can handle just about anything that comes your way. Having a repertoire of comeback responses and a good sense of when and with whom to use them is a very strong start.

I've coached, trained, and taught thousands of people, and what they say when I meet them again is how much better their work lives are because they've learned better ways to respond in tough situations. It's like having a set of special tools that many other people don't have. You don't drive to work dreading what someone might say to you. You're more ready now.

Getting to that point is possible, and it's just a matter of experimenting and making yourself aware of your comfort zone, and of what kinds of comebacks are effective where you work, with specific people, and in specific situations. Listen to what the more savvy people say when put on the spot. Understand that you don't need to become like them or use their kinds of comebacks, but consider whether the ones you've been using until now might be missing the mark, given the work culture.

Clearly, feeling out of control or pushed around at the workplace will seriously affect your happiness and success there, and as the stories in this book have shown, solving the problem provides tangible results and improves quality of life. Indeed, "If only I'd said" moments can be anxiety-producing and frustrating, and our goal throughout this book has been to help you reduce the number of them in your life. As a result, you should now know a lot more about yourself as a communicator and be able to respond on the spot if need be. With the R-List and other strategies you've learned, along with the review in chapter 10, you should feel inclined to experiment with comebacks you haven't used before.

Now, perhaps where you work there's no need to leave your comeback comfort zone to get through each day. Unlike Rachel Rongwhey, you may not have people around you who say what they don't mean or mean what they don't say. If so, you're in a rare and beautiful place and the rest of us would like to stop by, if not work there.

Even so, I just wouldn't get too comfortable, because workplaces—especially in turbulent economies—change frequently. No matter your age or stage, bosses leave, atmospheres change, and new rivalries develop. If you're young, you may not be a threat yet. In the future, you likely will be. It's good to be ready. If you're near the end of your career, new generations of employees with different communication styles are rapidly bumping up against you. Either way, making sure people understand that you will stand up for yourself at work, in conversation and in action, is crucial to your success—so keep practicing comebacks, even if you're fortunate enough to be in a good situation right now.

On the flip side, if you work for a company with a highly political or pathological culture, you're now ready to assume that 75 percent or more control over your situation and create your own space where things are better. You don't have to be the target anymore—not if you've been practicing comebacks and learning what works for you. Your enhanced skill will keep people with your worst interests at heart at bay.

Sure, you'll make mistakes, but before you know it you'll be ready for whatever comes at you. People will not walk all over you and expect to get away with it. You'll be telling them a thing or two even if pleasantly so. And just knowing you have that capacity is a very comforting thing.

One final thought: The strategies you've learned here aren't just for work. They're useful everywhere you go. And so, practicing at the supermarket, at the doctor's office, and so on, gets you ready for handling whatever comes your way. You can breathe a bit easier going out into the world each day now that you're well on your way to managing what happens to you. For example, just recently I was at an event having nothing to do with work and I was introduced to a woman as "a writer and artist." She replied, "Anyone can be a writer, so it's good you can do something else." Needless to say, I found that comment a bit odd. I might have said any number of defensive things or asked her if she was from another planet. "Do you really think we can all write?" I asked, smiling. She replied, "Oh, I mean we all learn to write, don't we? But you do other things, too, so that's great." Now, I don't know about you, but this was still strange. However, I'd just been introduced to her by a very pleasant woman who was looking a bit perplexed by what her friend had just said, so I figured I wouldn't gain anything by prolonging her agony. I said, "Interesting observation." She smiled and added, "Yes, I've always thought this way." We left it at that. Better to bring the whole thing to a happy ending and move on. Some moments and some days are just like that and there's no use making them worse.

Every day is an adventure in terms of what people say to each other. It's good to know when to just enjoy the ride and when to step in and make some alterations in its course. When you know how to do both, at work and elsewhere, you're in control and few things take you totally by surprise—and that is indeed a gift.

ACKNOWLEDGMENTS

Our thanks to all those people who shared their personal experiences and stories for *Comebacks at Work* through interviews or conversations, or simply in passing. The situations they described were difficult ones, often tricky and sometimes embarrassing—the kinds of interactions that can be tough on a person to recall, review, and analyze, but they did all three.

We especially thank Matt Inman, our wonderful editor at HarperCollins, for his dedication and hard work since the very moment he became involved with *Comebacks*. Not only has it been a pleasure working with Matt, we were also constantly impressed with his creativity and professionalism. We wish to express our deep gratitude to Hollis Heimbouch, Harper Business publisher and vice president, for her interest in working with Kathleen and her fascination with the concept for this book—we thank her as well for her inspiration and stewardship along the way.

Thanks once again to agent extraordinaire Peter Ginsberg. This is the fifth book Peter has worked on with Kathleen, and each journey has been a success due to his energy and creative insight as well as his strong involvement. As Buzz Lightyear might say: "From inception and beyond!"

At HarperCollins we would also like to thank several talented people who made this book possible. Among them Angie Lee, Nicole Reardon, Mark Ferguson, Kyle Hansen, and Annie Weiss.

Finally, we would also like to thank Ralph DeVito, Richard Bromfield, John D'Alton, Kevin Reardon, and several others—who know who they are but must remain unnamed—for their invaluable friendship, ideas, and encouragement.

NOTES

CHAPTER 2: GETTING STARTED

1. Jules Rotter, "Generalized Expectancies for Internal versus External Control of Reinforcements." *Psychological Monographs: General & Applied*, Vol. 80(1), 1966, pp.1–28.

CHAPTER 3: ASSESSING YOUR BASELINE COMEBACK SKILL

1. Deborah Solomon, "In Praise of Bad Art," *NYTimes.com*, January 24, 1999. Accessed (March 15, 2010) at: http://www.nytimes.com/1999/01/24/magazine/in-praise-of-bad-art.html?sec=&spon=&pagewanted=all.

2. "The Art of Illustration: A Cultural Context," *Rockwell Center for American Visual Studies*. Accessed (March 15, 2010) at: http:www.rcavs.org/art-of-illustration/.

3. "Snappy Insults, Funny Remarks," *geocities.com*. Accessed (January 12, 2009) at: http://www.geocities.com/freecooljokes/insults1.html.

4. Joan Rees, *Jane Austen: Woman and Writer* (New York: St. Martin's Press, 1976), pp. 49–50.

5. Ted Turner with Bill Burke, *Call Me Ted* (New York: Grand Central Publishing, 2008), p. 286.

6. http://today.msnbc.msn.com/id/17362505/.

CHAPTER 4: THE PERILS OF PATTERNS

1. Chris Argyris, "Good Communication That Blocks Learning," *Harvard Business Review*, July–August 1994, p. 80.

2. Kathleen K. Reardon, *They Don't Get It, Do They? Communication in the Workplace—Closing the Gap Between Women and Men* (New York: Little, Brown and Company, 1995).

3. Vernon E. Cronen, W. Barnett Pearce, and Lonna M. Snavely, "A Theory of Rule-Structure and Types of Episodes and a Study of Perceived Enmeshment in Undesired Repetitive Patterns ('URPs')," in Dan Nimmo, ed., *Communication Yearbook 3* (New Brunswick, New Jersey: Transaction Books, 1979), pp. 225–40; Paul Watzlawick, Don Jackson and Janet Beavin, *Pragmatics of Human Communication: A Study of Interactional Patterns, Pathologies and Paradoxes* (New York: W. W. Norton & Co., 1967); Kathleen K. Reardon, *They Don't Get It, Do They?* (New York: Little, Brown, 1995).

4. Kathleen K. Reardon, "Episodic Deviation: A Precursor to Dynamic Homeostasis," unpublished dissertation, University of Massachusetts–Amherst, 1978.

5. Michael Dobbs, *Madeleine Albright: A Twentieth-Century Odyssey* (New York: Henry Holt and Company, 1999), p. 252.

6. Ibid., p. 253.

7. Ibid.

8. Ibid., p. 257.

9. Aristotle, *The Ethics of Aristotle* (London: Penguin Classics, revised edition, 1976), pp.192–93.

10. Watzlawick, Jackson, Beavin, *Pragmatics of Human Communication*.

CHAPTER 5: OVERCOMING COMEBACK BRAIN FREEZE

1. Kathleen Kelley Reardon, *The Secret Handshake: Mastering the Politics of the Business Inner Circle* (New York: Currency, Doubleday, 2000).

2. Baldwin M. Way, Shelley E. Taylor, and Naomi I. Eisenberger, "Variation in the Mu-Opioid Receptor Gene (Oprm1) Is Associated with Dispositional and Neural Sensitivity to Social Rejection," *Proceedings of the National Academy of Sciences*, September 1, 2009, 106, no. 35, pp. 15079–84. Also: http://sciencedaily.com/releases/2009/08/090817142859.htm. Accessed May 3, 2010.

3. "It's Not All in Your Head: Descending Neural Mechanisms of Placebo-Induced Pain Control," *ScienceDaily.com*, August 29, 2009. Accessed (March 15, 2010) at: http://www.sciencedaily.com/releases/2009/08/090826152548.htm.

4. Roy F. Baumeister et al., "Social Rejection Can Reduce Pain and Increase Spending: Further Evidence That Money, Pain, and Belongingness Are Interrelated," *Psychological Inquiry*, 19: 2008, p. 146.

5. George Lakoff, *The Political Mind: Why You Can't Understand 21st-Century American Politics with an 18th-Century Brain* (New York: Viking Press, 2008).

6. Malcolm Gladwell, *The Tipping Point: How Little Things Can Make a Big Difference* (New York: Little, Brown and Company, 2000).

7. Glen H. Myers, "Metaphors at Work Hitting a High Note," *Boston Globe*, Boston.com, September 16, 2007. Accessed (March 15, 2010) at: http://www.boston.com/jobs/news/articles/2007/09/16/metaphors_at_work_hitting_a_high_note/.

CHAPTER 6: CHOOSING A *RELEVANT* COMEBACK

1. Kathleen Kelley Reardon, *The Secret Handshake* (New York: Currency, Doubleday, 2000).

CHAPTER 7: THE GUT CHECK

1. Carol Smith, "No Doubts: Women Are Better Managers," NYTimes .com, July 25, 2009. Accessed (March 15, 2010) at: http://www .nytimes.com/2009/07/26/business/26corner.html?pagewanted=1&_ r=2&em&adxnnlx=1248782525-Od8boAA5DIJeJleVCcXTMA.

2. Benedict Carey, "In Battle, Hunches Prove to Be Valuable," *New York Times*, July 28, 2009, p. A1.

3. Stanley Schachter, "The Interaction of Cognitive and Physiological Determinants of Emotional States," in Leonard Berkowitz, ed., *Advances in Experimental Social Psychology* (New York: Academic Press, 1964).

4. Paul Ekman, *Telling Lies: Clues to Deceit in the Marketplace, Politics, and Marriage,* 3rd edition (New York: Norton, 2001).

5. Jonah Lehrer, *How We Decide* (Boston and New York: Houghton Mifflin Harcourt, 2009), p. 25.

6. "American Idol," *Diane Magazine* (published by Curve fitness centers), summer 2008, 5, issue 2, p. 29.

7. Tana French, *In The Woods* (New York: Penguin Books, 2007), p. 356.

8. Jerome Groopman, *How Doctors Think* (New York: Houghton Mifflin Company, 2007), p. 8.

CHAPTER 8: WHEN CONFLICT IS INEVITABLE

1. Michael J. Fox, *Always Looking Up: The Adventures of an Incurable Optimist* (New York: Hyperion, 2009).

2. Barbara Peck, "Ginsberg Dazzles," *All Rise Magazine*, summer 2009, pp. 14–21.

3. Carol Smith, "No Doubts: Women Are Better Managers," *NYTimes.com,* July 25, 2009. Accessed (March 15, 2010) at: http://www

.nytimes.com/2009/07/26/business/26corner.html?pagewanted=1&_r=2&em&adxnnlx=1248782525-Od8boAA5DIJeJleVCcXTMA.

4. "Susan Boyle—singer—Britain's Got Talent 2009," YouTube.com, April 11, 2009. Accessed (March 15, 2010) at: http://www.youtube.com/watch?v=9lp0IWv8QZY.

5. Erving Goffman, *Behavior in Public Places* (New York: Free Press/Simon & Schuster, 1963), p. 110.

6. Matt Lauer interview with Vice President Joseph Biden, *Today*, MSNBC, August 28, 2009. Accessed (August 28, 2009) at: www.msnbc.msn/cp,/id/21134540/vp/325780#32578580.

7. Ibid.

8. Jim Lehrer, "Debating Our Destiny: Ronald Reagan Interview, August 7, 1989," September 9, 2008. Accessed (March 15, 2010) at: http://www.pbs.org/newshour/debatingourdestiny/interviews/reagan.html.

9. Chuck Raasch, "Former President Ronald Reagan Dies at 93," *USA Today.com*, June 5, 2004. Accessed (March 15, 2010) at: http://www.usatoday.com/news/washington/2004-06-05-reagan-obit_x.htm.

CHAPTER 9: PULSING THE OTHER PERSON

1. Mary Catherine Bateson, "Embracing Continuity and Change: The Power of Lifelong Learning," plenary session presentation, International Communication Association Conference, Chicago, May 28, 1999.

2. Earvin "Magic" Johnson, with William Novack, *My Life* (New York: Random House, 1992), p. 121.

3. Ibid., p. 101.

4. See Kathleen K. Reardon, *The Secret Handshake: Mastering the Politics of the Business Inner Circle.* (New York: Currency, Doubleday), 2000.

5. Robert Cialdini, *Influence: The Psychology of Persuasion* (New York: Collins Business Essentials), 2006.

CHAPTER 10: ASSESSING THE SITUATION

1. Robert Mayer, *How to Win Any Argument: Without Raising Your Voice, Losing Your Cool, or Coming to Blows* (Franklin Lakes, New Jersey: Career Press, 2005), p. 42.

2. Ibid., p. 41.

INDEX

ABOUT THE AUTHORS

Kathleen Kelley Reardon, PhD, is a professor of management at the Marshall School of Business at USC, a consultant and speaker at such major corporations as Pfizer, Siemens, Epson, IBM, News Corporation, and Toyota, and one of HuffingtonPost.com's signature and top bloggers, whose writing is frequently picked up and featured on Yahoo. She has appeared on *Good Morning America* with Charlie Gibson and Nancy Snyderman, *NBC Nightly News*, *The Today Show*, and Bloomberg. She is the author of nine books, including *The Secret Handshake*, *It's All Politics*, and *The Skilled Negotiator*. Dr. Reardon is also a distinguished fellow of First Star, an organization that advocates for the rights and education of children at risk. She lives in Rhode Island, where she is a painter and novelist.

Christopher T. Noblet is a freelance writer and editor with a background in speech writing and public affairs. He has an MA from the University of Connecticut and an international MBA from the University of Southern California. He also lives in Rhode Island, writes for *Audiophile Voice* magazine, and is an audiophile himself and a guitarist.